OECD Sovereign Borrowing Outlook 2016

This work is published on the responsibility of the Secretary-General of the OECD. The opinions expressed and arguments employed herein do not necessarily reflect the official views of the Organisation or of the governments of its member countries.

This document and any map included herein are without prejudice to the status of or sovereignty over any territory, to the delimitation of international frontiers and boundaries and to the name of any territory, city or area.

Please cite this publication as:
OECD (2016), *OECD Sovereign Borrowing Outlook 2016*, OECD Publishing, Paris.
http://dx.doi.org/10.1787/sov_b_outlk-2016-en

ISBN 978-92-64-25730-6 (print)
ISBN 978-92-64-25731-3 (PDF)

Series: OECD Sovereign Borrowing Outlook
ISSN 2306-0468 (print)
ISSN 2306-0476 (online)

The statistical data for Israel are supplied by and under the responsibility of the relevant Israeli authorities. The use of such data by the OECD is without prejudice to the status of the Golan Heights, East Jerusalem and Israeli settlements in the West Bank under the terms of international law.

Photo credits: © Inmagine/Designpics.

Corrigenda to OECD publications may be found on line at: *www.oecd.org/about/publishing/corrigenda.htm*.

Foreword

The 2016 edition of the OECD Sovereign Borrowing Outlook *provides data, information and background on sovereign borrowing needs and discusses funding strategies and debt management policies for OECD countries and the OECD area, including:*

- *Gross borrowing requirements.*
- *Net borrowing requirements.*
- *Central government marketable debt.*
- *Interactions between fiscal policy, public debt management and monetary policy.*
- *Funding strategies, procedures and instruments.*
- *Impact of new regulations on primary market operations.*
- *Liquidity in secondary markets.*
- *Transparency of public debt statistics, operations and policies.*

Each year, the OECD's Bond Market and Public Debt Management Unit circulates a survey on the borrowing needs of OECD governments. The responses are compiled and incorporated into the OECD Sovereign Borrowing Outlook *to provide regular updates on trends and developments associated with sovereign borrowing requirements, funding strategies, market infrastructure and debt levels from the perspective of public debt managers. The* Outlook *makes a policy distinction between funding strategy and borrowing requirements. The central government marketable gross borrowing needs, or requirements, are calculated on the basis of budget deficits and redemptions. The funding strategy entails decisions on how borrowing needs are going to be financed using different instruments (e.g. long-term, short-term, nominal, indexed, etc.) and which distribution channels (auctions, tap, syndication, etc.) are being used.*

Comments and questions should be addressed to the Bond Markets and Public Debt Management Unit (e-mail: Publicdebt@oecd.org). Find out more about OECD work on bond markets and public debt management online at www.oecd.org/finance/public-debt/.

Acknowledgements

The Sovereign Borrowing Outlook is part of the activities of the OECD Working Party on Public Debt Management, incorporated in the programme of work of the Bond Market and Public Debt Management Unit within the Financial Affairs Division of the OECD Directorate for Financial and Enterprise Affairs. This publication was prepared by: Sebastian Schich (who drafted Chapter 1); Hans J. Blommestein (who drafted Chapters 2, 3 and 4); and Perla Ibarlucea Flores and Romain Despalins (who provided statistical support for all chapters). The Transparency Task Force members Thomas Olofsson (Chair; DMO, Sweden); Wendy Chang (Central Bank, Canada); Ove Jensen (DMO/Central Bank, Denmark); Sturla Palsson and Hafsteinn Hafsteinsson (Central Bank, Iceland); Fatos Koc (Treasury, Turkey) contributed to Chapter 4. Timothy Bishop coordinated and provided comments on all chapters. Edward Smiley provided invaluable publishing guidance.

Table of contents

Tables

Figures

Acronyms and abbreviations

AFT	Agence France Trésor
AKK	Hungarian Debt Management Agency
AOFM	Australian Office of Financial Management
APF	Asset Purchase Facility Operations
APP	Asset Purchase Programme
ATM	Average Time to Maturity
ATR	Average Time to Re-fixing
BOE	Bank of England
BOJ	Bank of Japan
BSRD	Bangko Sentral Registration Document
BTP	Buono del Tesoro Poliennale
CACs	Collective Active Clauses
CAPM	Capital Asset Pricing Model
CBs	Central Banks
CCPs	Central Counterparties
CDS	Credit Default Swap
CRAs	Credit Rating Agencies
CSDR	Central Securities Depositories Regulation
CY	Calendar Year
DDA	Dutch Direct Auction
DMOs	Debt Management Offices
DSL	Dutch State Loan
DTC	Dutch Treasury Certificates
ECB	European Central Bank
EFSF	European Financial Stability Facility
EFSM	European Financial Stabilisation Mechanism
EMIR	European Markets Infrastructure Regulation
EMTN	Euro Medium Term Note
ESM	European Stability Mechanism
EU	European Union
FAS	Fiscal Authorities
FED	Federal Reserve
FRAs	Forward Rate Agreements
FRBNY	Federal Reserve Bank of New York
FRNs	Floating Rate Notes
FTT	Financial Transactions Tax
GBR	Gross Borrowing Requirement
GDP	Gross Domestic Product

GEMMs	Gilt-edged Market Makers
IFAC	International Federation of Accountants
IGCP	Portuguese Treasury and Debt Management Agency
IMF	International Monetary Fund
IPSAS	International Public Sector Accounting Standards
JGB	Japanese Government Bond
LCR	Liquidity Coverage Ratio
LHS	Left Hand Side
LSAP	Large Scale Asset Purchase
LTROs	Longer-term Refinancing Operations
MEP	Maturity Extension Programme
MPE	Multiple Point of Entry
MTDS	Medium Term Debt Strategies
NBR	Net Borrowing Requirement
NSFR	Net Stable Funding Ratio
NTMA	National Treasury Management Agency
NZDMO	New Zealand Debt Management Office
OECD	Organisation for Economic Co-operation and Development
OLO	Obligations Linéaires Ordinaires
OMT	Outright Monetary Transactions
ONS	Office for National Statistics
OSI	Official Sector Involvement
PDM	Public Debt Management
PDs	Primary Dealers
PPPs	Public-Private Partnerships
PSI	Private Sector Involvement
QE	Quantitative Easing
RBNZ	Reserve Bank of New Zealand
RHS	Right Hand Side
RWAs	Risk Weighted Assets
SMP	Securities Market Programme
SNA	System of National Accounts
SOMA	System Open Market Account
SPFA	Slovenian Public Finance Act
TIPS	Treasury Inflation-Protected Securities
TTF	Transparency Task Force
WB	World Bank
WPDM	Working Party on Public Debt Management

Editorial

Although government borrowing requirements have declined slightly, debt ratios remain elevated and redemption profiles challenging

The *OECD Sovereign Borrowing Outlook 2016* (the *Outlook*) indicates that the combined gross borrowing needs of governments have declined gradually in recent years, thanks to tighter fiscal policies. Nevertheless, net borrowing requirements are still positive and fiscal consolidation efforts have slowed in response to fragile economic growth. As a result, central government debt to GDP ratios in OECD countries remains above 70% (and close to 90% in G7 countries). This remains high by historical standards, despite a slight decline in 2015 and estimated decline in 2016.

Previous editions of the *Outlook* highlighted the challenging redemption profiles. Updated estimations of medium-term maturity projections confirm the importance of roll-over risk. The *Outlook* shows that more than a third of total outstanding long-term debt and close to 45% of total debt in 2015 will mature over the three years from 2015 to 2018. While sovereign debt dynamics are still fragile, this situation highlights the critical role of risk management in debt management strategies.

Evolving market structures and conditions bring new challenges and opportunities for sovereign issuers

Eight years after the onset of the global crisis, sovereign issuers in OECD countries continue to face the challenges presented by evolving market structures and conditions. The combined effect of unconventional monetary policies, expansionary fiscal policies and exits from those policies as well as post-crisis regulatory reforms have had a significant impact on sovereign debt markets in OECD countries.

The *Outlook* indicates that many sovereign issuers have observed structural changes in sovereign bond markets, particularly regarding market liquidity, investor demand and trade practices. The surveys highlight growing concerns amongst some debt management offices (DMOs) over low market liquidity due to the unintended consequences of regulatory reforms and unconventional monetary policies. Also, the increased presence of public sector investors – as large central banks have become dominant holders of sovereign debt – has contributed to this trend, as many of them use buy-and-hold strategies in their investment decisions. In general, liquid government bond markets support financial markets because of the important benchmark role played by marketable government debt. Strong liquidity in secondary markets also improves sovereign borrowing conditions in primary markets, particularly by lowering the borrowing costs of new issuances. In addition to liquidity conditions, sovereign debt managers have also observed a structural change in trade practices. Specifically, the proportion of trades conducted electronically is rising over time, although the net impact of "electronification" on government bond markets requires further analysis.

The survey of primary markets revealed that many DMOs employed their operational toolbox to cope with the augmented challenges. That is, they adjusted their issuance strategies, sales procedures and offerings of debt instruments in accordance with evolving market structures. While addressing the challenges, sovereign issuers have for instance issued long-term debt, seizing the opportunity to extend their yield curve at exceptionally low interest rates.

Low interest rates: A blessing -or a curse- for sovereign borrowers?

This edition of the *Outlook* sheds light on the implications of low interest rates for government bond markets. The 2015 *OECD Business and Finance Outlook* focused on the implications of a very low interest rate environment and discussed the outlook for pension funds and life insurance companies. From a debt managers' perspective, a low interest rate environment eases the trade-off between cost and risk parameters of different instrument choices. Furthermore, a flattened yield curve implies a low expected cost of long maturities, which in turn presents an opportunity for low-cost mitigation of roll-over risk. Therefore, several OECD DMOs have issued long dated (sometimes ultra-long dated) securities and lengthened redemption profiles.

On the other hand, declining long-term bond yields – even to negative territory in several OECD countries – raise concerns regarding investors' balance sheets. If sustained for a prolonged period, the low interest rate environment might impair institutional investor demand – pension funds and insurance companies – for government securities, particularly for long-dated indexed bonds. Furthermore, with continuing bond purchase programmes of large central banks and rising demand from other public institutions, secondary market trading activities might shrink further, which in turn could have negative implications for market volatility.

Looking ahead, as the structure of financial markets continues to evolve, the principles of debt management – including flexibility in market operations, communications with investors and other stakeholders, predictability and transparency – will remain critical hallmarks of government debt management. Particularly, while central banks' policies are expected to dominate financial markets, consultation between central banks and sovereign debt managers, as their respective mandates imply that they operate in the same markets, continues to be important.

Adrian Blundell-Wignall
Director, OECD Directorate for Financial
and Enterprise Affairs

Executive summary

While sovereign borrowing requirements have slightly declined, redemption profiles remain challenging. Sovereign debt ratios are still high by historical standards in OECD countries.

Sovereign borrowing in the OECD area, which had risen rapidly as result of the policy response to the global financial crisis, has declined owing to fiscal consolidation. However, net borrowing remains positive. The level of sovereign debt against the backdrop of slowdown in real activity remains high by historical standards. Surveys of the outlook for borrowing indicate that aggregate central government marketable debt across the OECD will rise slowly but steadily and exceed USD 40 trillion in 2016.

Redemption profiles of outstanding medium- and long-term central government debt remain challenging over the next few years. In order to address roll-over risk, debt managers aim to lengthen and smooth out the redemption profile. Such a strategy tends to involve higher debt-servicing costs over the short term, given that yield curves are generally upward sloping. At the same time, it makes debt-servicing costs more predictable, and this advantage is currently achieved at limited cost because of the low interest rate environment. Therefore, funding strategies of many Debt Management Offices (DMOs) have leaned steadily on long-term local currency financing instruments.

Secondary market liquidity has remained an important source of concern for debt managers

From a debt management perspective, liquidity in financial markets is important for the cost of borrowing. Also, strong liquidity is essential for a government bond market to provide reliable and efficient price signals for other financial markets, even in times of market dislocation or stress. Since the onset of the global financial crisis, unconventional monetary policies, new regulations and structural changes in the investor base have affected the liquidity of government bond markets. DMOs are addressing the issue of liquidity risk by stepping up their efforts to monitor liquidity indicators, putting in place several measures to better evaluate and motivate dealer performance in market-making, and adapting their own issuance strategies.

Debt managers' perspectives regarding the implications of the regulatory changes in the financial system (Basel III, Solvency II, CACs, MiFID II, Dodd-Frank Act, etc.) for the functioning of the primary markets suggest that these new regulations could put more pressure on dealers' balance sheets and adversely affect market liquidity and the demand for government securities. However, it is difficult to quantify their full impact on primary markets of government bonds at this stage. In response to regulatory changes and their impacts, debt managers have recently made changes to issuing strategies, procedures and techniques. Most debt offices have increased the frequency of auctions, while some of them introduced a post-auction option facility and mini-tenders to investors.

Debt managers continue to witness structural changes in the investor base for government securities which also has an impact on secondary market liquidity. Particularly, the importance of public sector institutions as investors in sovereign bonds has increased over the last decade. This development has been driven by a combination of factors: i) quantitative easing programmes; ii) the substantial accumulation of foreign exchange reserves; and iii) risk-averse investment strategies of growing sovereign wealth funds. Public sector institutions are generally perceived as being a more stable investor group than private investors. However, the increased share of public sector investors raises concerns about concentration risk and market liquidity. Against this backdrop, debt managers recognise the importance of a diversified investor base, and have focused on attracting investors with different mandates and investment horizons through issuance strategies and investor relations policies.

Additional pressure from investors and other stakeholders to increase the transparency of debt management operations and policies

Since the onset of the global financial and economic crisis and the associated huge increase in sovereign borrowing operations, governments have been facing additional pressure from investors and other stakeholders to increase the transparency of operations and policies. Enhanced transparency of strategies, operations and policies for public debt management reduces investor uncertainty, thereby increasing the attractiveness of government bond markets. This in turn broadens the investor base, lowers risk premiums and eases borrowing costs. However, maximum transparency may not be the ideal strategic objective for a DMO, due to the potential for reduced flexibility and overly-complex information.

Against this backdrop, the OECD Task Force on Transparency of Debt Statistics, Operations and Policies examined current data dissemination practices and developed concrete recommendations to those managing government debts. The Task Force highlighted the importance of regular and timely publication of debt statistics. This Task Force also stressed that debt managers should give careful consideration to intelligibility and accessibility features when disclosing information regarding debt statistics, operations and policies.

Key findings

- Net borrowing requirements have continued to decline from their peaks of 2008 and 2009 and gross borrowing requirements from their peak of 2012.
- The share of long-term bonds in issuance operations has been increasing in recent years and it is expected to reach 59% in 2016, almost 10 percentage points higher compared to 2007 and 2008. This change in the borrowing structure has lengthened the average maturity of outstanding marketable central government debt.
- The share of long-term debt is estimated to exceed 90% of total central government marketable debt in 2016.
- More than a third of total outstanding long-term debt in the OECD area in 2015 is expected to mature over the three years from 2015 to 2018.

Chapter 1

Sovereign borrowing outlook for OECD countries

This chapter examines sovereign borrowing needs in OECD countries from 2007 to 2016. It first looks at the net and gross borrowing needs of OECD governments in the context of ongoing fiscal consolidation. It then considers recent trends in central government marketable debt in the OECD and general government debt ratios for selected OECD countries, as well as current interest rates and the possible medium to long-term effect of negative interest rates. Finally, the chapter examines the relationship between monetary policy and debt management decisions, the role of public institutions as investors in sovereign bonds and growing concerns about secondary market liquidity.

The statistical data for Israel are supplied by and under the responsibility of the relevant Israeli authorities. The use of such data by the OECD is without prejudice to the status of the Golan Heights, East Jerusalem and Israeli settlements in the West Bank under the terms of international law.

1.1. Introduction

This chapter* examines net and gross sovereign borrowing in OECD countries for 2007 to 2016. It first looks at the net and gross borrowing needs of OECD governments in the context of fiscal developments. It then considers recent trends in central government marketable debt in the OECD area, central government debt ratios for groups of selected OECD countries and general government gross financial liabilities government debt ratios a group of selected major OECD countries. The chapter then discusses current interest rates and the challenges arising over the medium to long-term from negative interest rates. Finally, the chapter examines the relationship between monetary policy and debt management decisions and the role of public institutions as investors in sovereign bonds.

Key findings

- Sovereign borrowing needs in the OECD area as a whole have declined, owing to fiscal consolidation efforts. Net borrowing requirements have continued to decline from their peaks attained in 2008/09 and gross borrowing requirements from their peaks attained in 2012.
- Net borrowing continues to be positive however and sovereign debt levels, which had risen rapidly as a result of the policy response to the global financial crisis and the real activity deceleration associated with it, continue to be high by historical standards.
- Interest rates are low and they are even sometimes negative for high-credit-quality sovereigns. This borrowing environment facilitates the servicing of debt and influences the perceived need to reduce high public debt levels.
- Looking ahead, purchases of government bonds by central bank and other public authorities that have constituted such a considerable share of sovereign bond demand are likely to decline, even if the outlook in this regard differs across regions.
- Redemption profiles remain challenging over the next few years. Debt management offices have been reacting to these challenges among other things by making sovereign debt reimbursement requirements as light as possible over the short to medium term. As part of such efforts, redemption profiles were lengthened, thus limiting rollover risks. Such a strategy tends to involve higher debt-servicing costs over the short term, given that yield curves are upward sloping. At the same time, it makes debt-servicing costs more predictable, and this advantage is currently achieved at limited costs.
- A survey among debt management offices that are members of the OECD Working Party on Debt Management revealed concerns among debt management offices regarding sovereign bond secondary market liquidity, especially in the case of bonds that are not "on-the run". These concerns are valid, and more research is needed to more fully

* This chapter was prepared by Sebastian Schich, Senior Economist, OECD Financial Affairs Division, with research and statistical support from Romain Despalins, Statistician, OECD Financial Affairs Division, and Perla Ibarlucea Flores, Statistician, OECD Financial Affairs Division.

understand the implications of the evolving sovereign bond market structures for liquidity, trading and risk management practises, and market monitoring.

1.2. Net and gross borrowing needs of OECD governments decline with fiscal consolidation

Net borrowing needs of OECD governments have continued to decline, reflecting progress regarding fiscal consolidation.[1] In fact, *OECD Economic Outlook* projections (OECD, 2015b) show an improvement in actual general government balances, from 5.1% of GDP in 2014 to an estimated 4.5% in 2015 and 4.2% in 2016.[2] This situation is reflected in central government marketable net borrowing requirements that have declined and are estimated to continue to decline.

The net central government borrowing requirement for the region as a whole is projected to return in 2016 to a level similar to the one observed before the global financial crisis (Figure 1.1). The financial crisis, and the policy response to it, implied a drastically increased additional borrowing requirement in the years 2008 and 2009. From its peak of USD 3.3 trillion attained in 2009, net central government marketable borrowing requirement has fallen to an expected USD 1.2 trillion in 2015. Looking further ahead, the borrowing needs of OECD central governments combined are expected to decline further to USD 600 billion in 2016 (Table 1.1).[3]

Figure 1.1. **Fiscal and borrowing outlook in OECD countries for the period 2007-16**

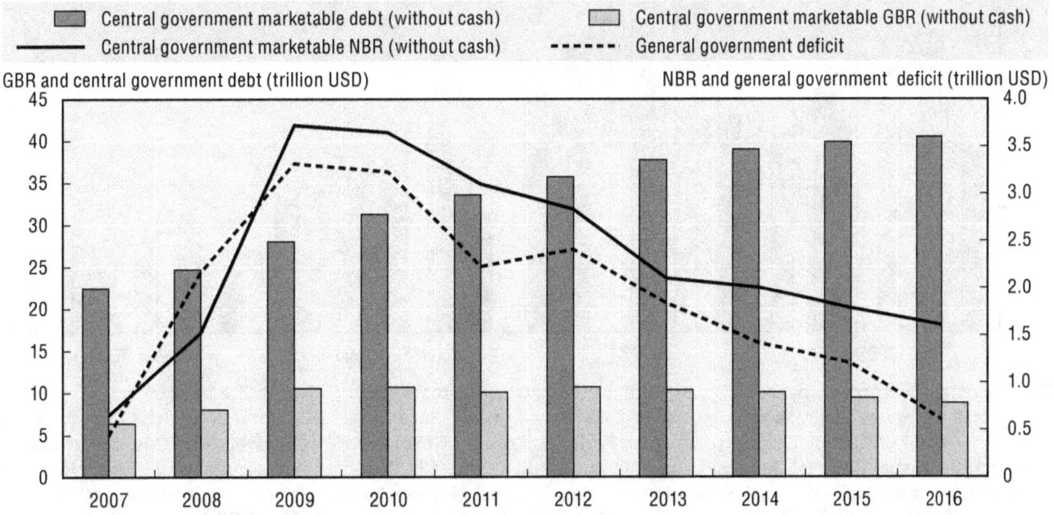

Note: GBR = gross borrowing requirement, NBR = net borrowing requirement. General government deficit is derived from the general government net lending as published in the *OECD Economic Outlook* No. 98 for all OECD countries except for Chile, Mexico and Turkey for which the source is the IMF World Economic Outlook (October 2015). Figures are calculated based on data in national currencies using exchange rates as of 1 December 2009.

Source: 2015 Survey on central government marketable debt and borrowing by the OECD Working Party on Debt Management; *OECD Economic Outlook* No. 98; IMF World Economic Outlook (October 2015); Bloomberg, national authorities' websites and OECD calculations.

StatLink http://dx.doi.org/10.1787/888933393035

Expressed as a percentage of GDP rather than in absolute amounts, aggregate borrowing numbers for the OECD area as a whole hide considerable differences across selected OECD groupings, with the group of G7 countries being characterised by relatively higher marketable gross borrowing requirements as of GDP than other OECD countries (Figure 1.2).

Table 1.1. **Central government marketable gross and net borrowing and marketable debt in the OECD area**

Trillion USD

	2007	2008	2009	2010	2011	2012	2013	2014	2015	2016
Central government marketable GBR (with cash)	6.9	8.6	11.0	11.2	10.6	11.2	10.8	10.6	9.9	9.3
Central government marketable GBR (without cash)	6.4	8.1	10.6	10.7	10.1	10.7	10.4	10.1	9.4	8.8
Central government marketable debt (without cash)	22.5	24.7	28.0	31.3	33.6	35.7	37.7	39.0	39.9	40.5
Central government marketable NBR (without cash)	0.4	2.2	3.3	3.2	2.2	2.4	1.8	1.4	1.2	0.6
General government deficit	0.7	1.5	3.7	3.6	3.1	2.8	2.1	2.0	1.8	1.6

Note: GBR = gross borrowing requirement, NBR = net borrowing requirement. General government deficit is derived from the general government net lending as published in the *OECD Economic Outlook* No. 98 for all OECD countries except for Chile, Mexico and Turkey for which the source is the IMF World Economic Outlook (October 2015). "Cash" refers to short-term instruments in the money market such as outstanding commercial paper or instruments for liquidity management; these instruments are either excluded ("without cash") or included ("with cash"). Figures are calculated based on data in national currencies using the exchange rates as of 1 December 2009.

Source: 2015 Survey on central government marketable debt and borrowing by the OECD Working Party on Debt Management; *OECD Economic Outlook* No. 98; IMF World Economic Outlook (October 2015); Bloomberg, national authorities' websites and OECD calculations.

StatLink http://dx.doi.org/10.1787/888933393233

Figure 1.2. **Central government marketable gross borrowing in OECD countries**

As a percentage of GDP

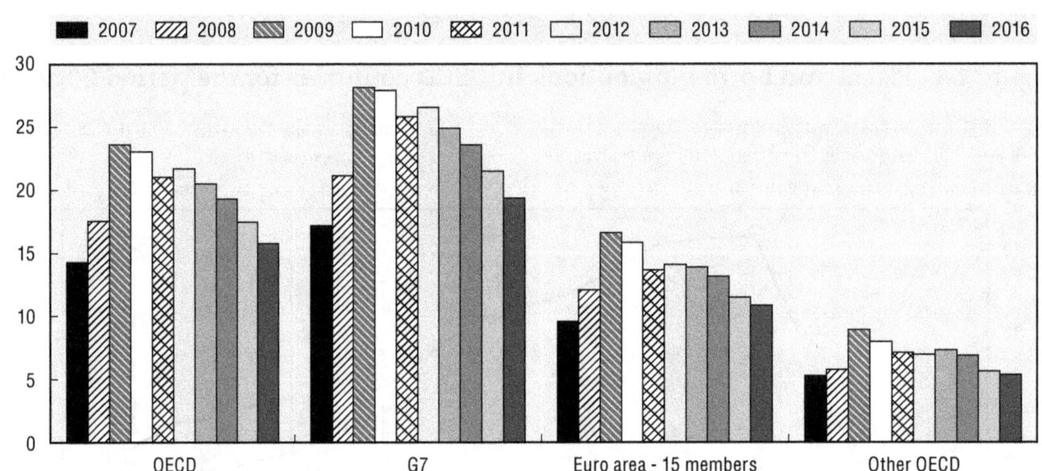

Note: Central government marketable GBR without cash. Values of marketable GBR and GDP have been aggregated by using fixed exchange rates, as of 1 December 2009, for all years. "Euro area – 15 members" includes the following OECD countries: Austria, Belgium, Estonia, Finland, France, Germany, Greece, Ireland, Italy, Luxembourg, Netherlands, Portugal, Slovak Republic, Slovenia and Spain. "Other OECD" includes Australia, Chile, Czech Republic, Denmark, Hungary, Iceland, Israel, Korea, Mexico, New Zealand, Norway, Poland, Sweden, Switzerland and Turkey.

Source: 2015 Survey on central government marketable debt and borrowing by the OECD Working Party on Debt Management; *OECD Economic Outlook* No. 98; Bloomberg, national authorities' websites and OECD calculations.

StatLink http://dx.doi.org/10.1787/888933393092

As foreshadowed in the 2014 edition of the *OECD Sovereign Borrowing Outlook*, gross borrowing needs of governments had peaked in 2012 (Table 1.1). The decline from 2012 to 2013 observed at the time of writing that edition has continued into 2015. The present chapter of this 2016 edition estimates that gross marketable borrowing requirements,[4] calculated on the basis of budget deficits and redemptions of marketable debt,[5] stands at USD 9.4 trillion in 2015, compared to USD 10.4 trillion two years earlier. It also projects gross marketable borrowing requirements to further decline to USD 8.8 trillion in 2016.[6] The effect of the global financial crisis on these various measures is thus diminishing, although only very gradually.

1.3. Central government marketable debt in the OECD area may not have peaked yet

Net borrowing in the OECD area as a whole continues to be positive, however, and this observation is reflected in the continued growth of central government marketable debt.[7] Figure 1.3 shows recent trends in central government marketable debt in the OECD area, based on data collected through a survey on central government marketable debt and borrowing by the OECD Working Party on Debt Management for the period from 2007 to 2016 (including OECD staff projections). The figure shows that a measure of aggregate central government marketable debt across the OECD area is estimated to rise slowly but steadily to exceed the equivalent of USD 40 trillion in 2016.

Such estimates of region-wide aggregates reflect the assumptions being made as to how to aggregate data in different national currencies to calculate area-wide aggregates. The estimates referred to above (and reported in previous editions of the *OECD Sovereign Borrowing Outlook*) are in fact based on the assumption of fixed exchange rates (as of 2009 values) to aggregate data across the different national currencies in the OECD area. This assumption facilitates the interpretation of developments in volumes over time and allows comparison of the volume data discussed in the present edition of the Sovereign Borrowing Outlook with those reported in previous editions.

Using varying foreign exchange rates instead to calculate area-wide aggregates, central government marketable debt is estimated to have peaked in 2013 at USD 35.6 trillion (Figure 1.3 Panel C). It is estimated to be equivalent to USD 33.9 trillion in 2016. Among other things, the differences in estimates depending on exchange rate assumptions (i.e. fixed versus flexible) reflect the depreciation of the Japanese Yen versus the USD. The depreciation in the bilateral exchange rate implies that Japanese central government marketable debt contributes less to area-wide aggregates expressed in USD.

Thus, metrics of marketable public debt in the OECD area suggest that it is high by historical standards for the period for which this data has been collected (that is, since 2007). That said, the reported numbers reflect the choice of exchange rate assumptions and, thus, absolute numbers expressed in any single currency should be interpreted with some caution.

Incidentally, the same caveat applies to the interpretation of aggregate data of gross borrowing in the area, which is discussed in Section 1.2. Considering flexible rather than fixed exchange rates when aggregating central government marketable gross borrowing across OECD countries, estimates for 2014 are USD 9.2 trillion (Figure 1.4). This number compares with estimates of USD 10.1 trillion for 2014 when considering fixed exchange rates instead, as reported in Table 1.1 (and in previous editions of the *OECD Sovereign Borrowing Outlook*).

Figure 1.3. **Central government marketable debt (without cash) in the OECD area**

Panel A. USD trillion considering different exchange rate assumptions in aggregation of national currency values

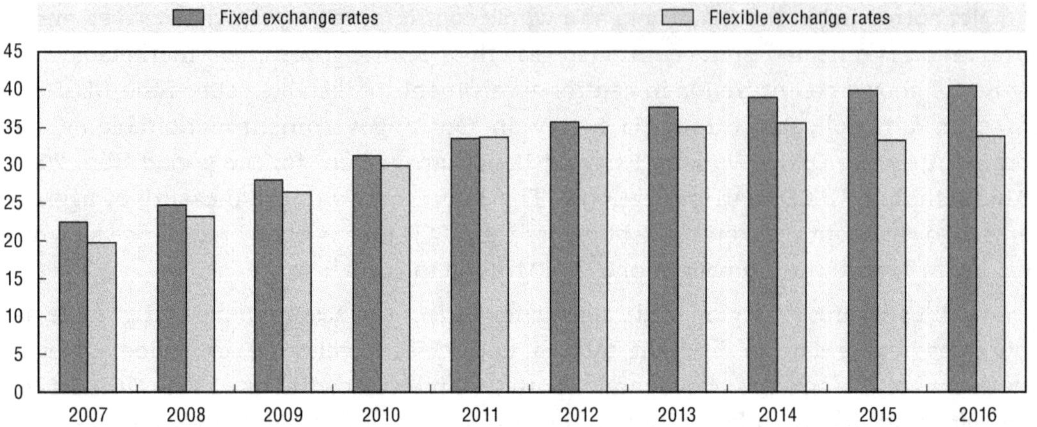

Panel B. USD trillion using fixed exchange rates in aggregation of national currency values

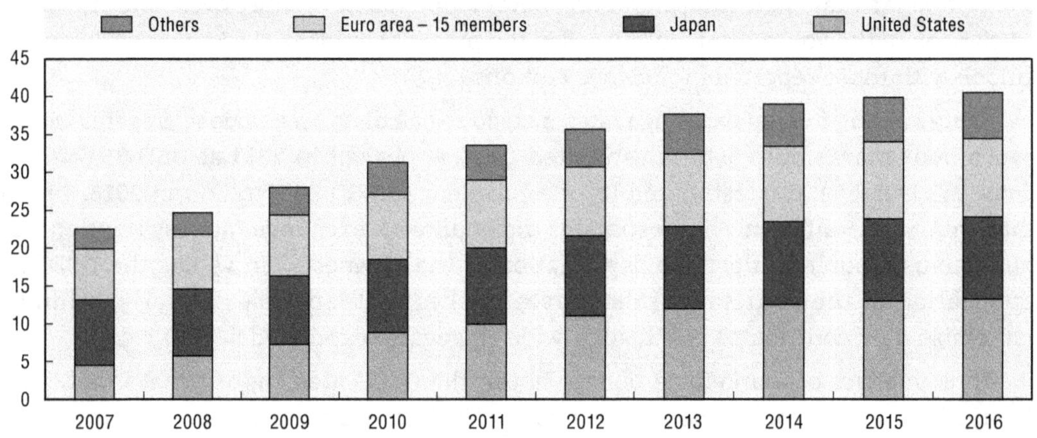

Panel C. USD trillion using flexible exchange rates in aggregation of national currency values

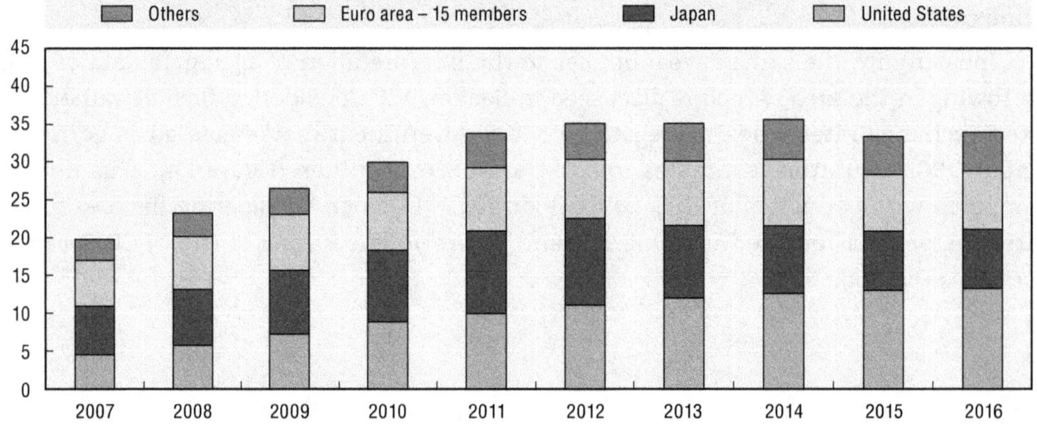

Note: Data aggregated using "fixed exchange rates" are calculated using exchange rates as of 1 December 2009. Data aggregated using "flexible exchange rates" are calculated using annual period average exchange rates. Euro area countries considered in this figure include Austria, Belgium, Estonia, Finland, France, Germany, Greece, Ireland, Italy, Luxembourg, Netherlands, Portugal, Slovak Republic, Slovenia and Spain.

Source: 2015 Survey on central government marketable debt and borrowing by the OECD Working Party on Debt Management.

StatLink http://dx.doi.org/10.1787/888933393109

Figure 1.4. **Central government marketable gross borrowing requirement (without cash) in the OECD area**

Panel A. USD trillion considering different exchange rate assumptions in aggregation of national currency values

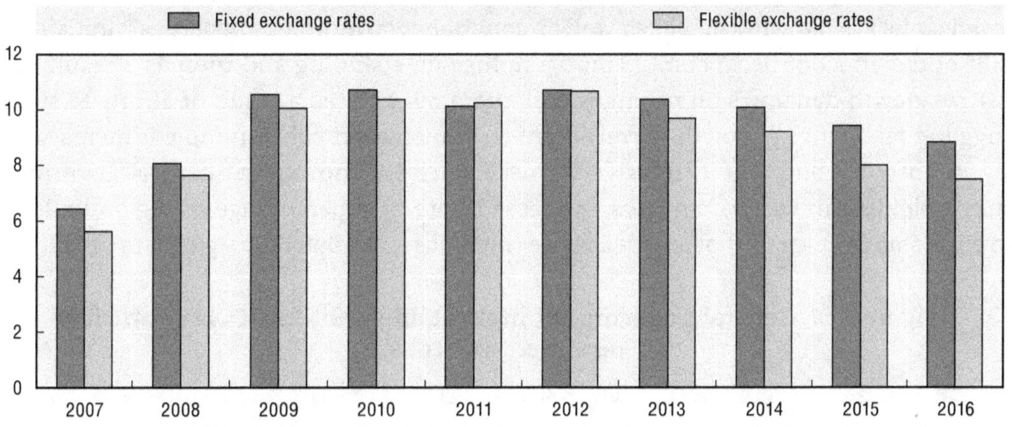

Panel B. USD trillion using fixed exchange rates in aggregation of national currency values

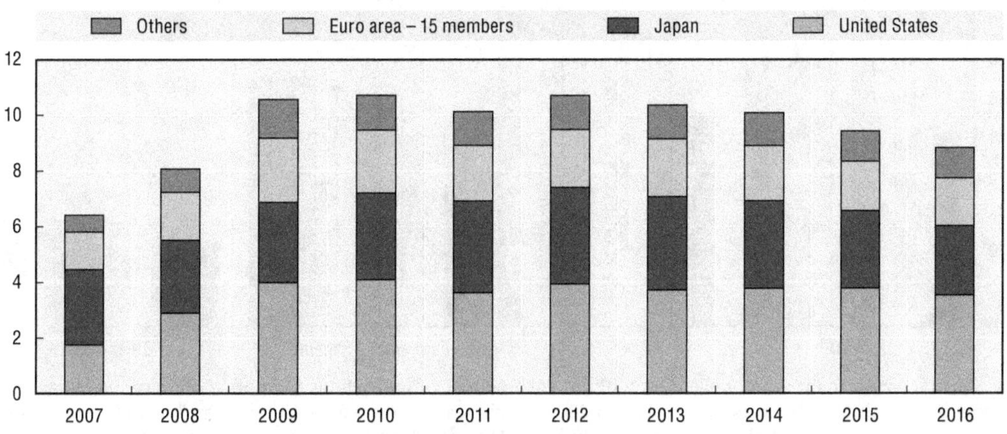

Panel C. USD trillion using flexible exchange rates in aggregation of national currency values

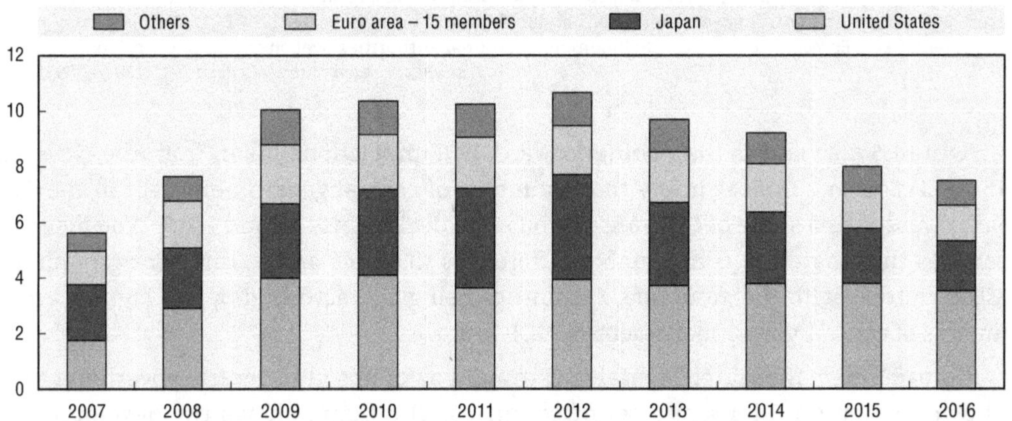

Note: Data aggregated using "fixed exchange rates" are calculated using exchange rates as of 1 December 2009. Data aggregated using "flexible exchange rates" are calculated using annual period average exchange rates. Euro area countries considered in this figure include Austria, Belgium, Estonia, Finland, France, Germany, Greece, Ireland, Italy, Luxembourg, Netherlands, Portugal, Slovak Republic, Slovenia and Spain.

Source: 2015 Survey on central government marketable debt and borrowing by the OECD Working Party on Debt Management.

StatLink http://dx.doi.org/10.1787/888933393119

1.4. Government debt ratios for selected OECD area groupings are close to historical peaks

The response of governments to the global financial crisis set the stage for a surge in fiscal deficits and growing actual as well as contingent government liabilities.[8] Initially, as a result of the effect of fiscal stimulus programmes on spending and then as a result of the negative growth dynamics on revenues and, more recently, as a result of efforts to support struggling real activity growth, government debt increased substantially. It increased not only in absolute but also in relative terms. Figure 1.5 shows that central government marketable debt in OECD countries, expressed here as a percentage of region-wide GDP, currently stands at levels that are well above those observed before the global financial crisis.

Figure 1.5. **Central government marketable debt in OECD countries**

(As a percentage of GDP)

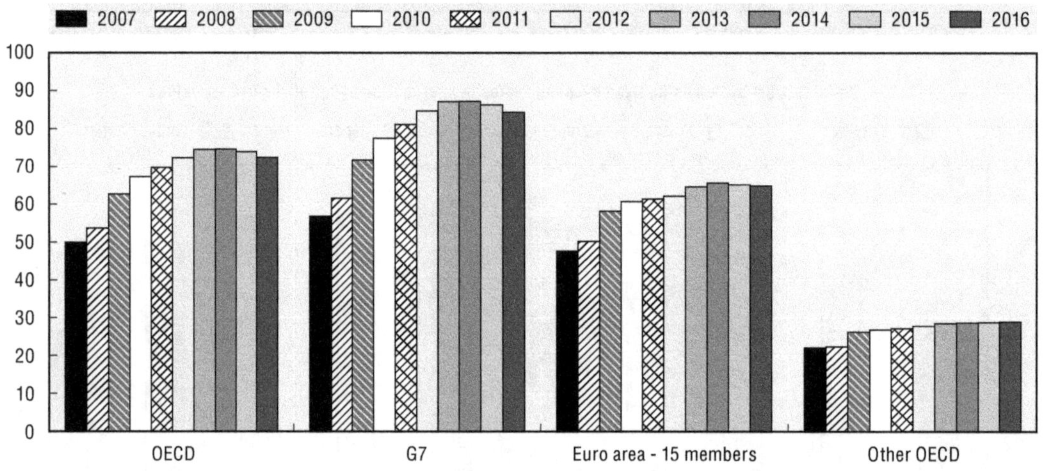

Note: Central government marketable debt without cash. Values of marketable debt and GDP have been aggregated by using fixed exchange rates, as of 1 December 2009, for all years. "Euro area – 15 members" includes the following OECD countries: Austria, Belgium, Estonia, Finland, France, Germany, Greece, Ireland, Italy, Luxembourg, Netherlands, Portugal, Slovak Republic, Slovenia and Spain. "Other OECD" include Australia, Chile, Czech Republic, Denmark, Hungary, Iceland, Israel, Korea, Mexico, New Zealand, Norway, Poland, Sweden, Switzerland and Turkey.

Source: 2015 Survey on central government marketable debt and borrowing by the OECD Working Party on Debt Management; *OECD Economic Outlook* No. 98; Bloomberg, national authorities' websites and OECD calculations.

StatLink http://dx.doi.org/10.1787/888933393122

Figure 1.5 also shows that, going forward, GDP projections taken from the November 2015 *OECD Economic Outlook* imply that estimates of central government debt in the OECD area (expressed as a share of GDP) are estimated to decline in 2015 and 2016.[9] The figure also illustrates that there are considerable differences in levels across different groupings of OECD countries, with the group of G7 countries being characterised by the highest average estimates of central-government-debt-to-GDP ratios.

A broader debt measure, general government as opposed to central government debt, is shown in Figure 1.6 for a sub-set of countries. The figure shows the development of general government gross financial liabilities expressed as a percentage of GDP for a group of selected OECD countries (which, incidentally, include all G7 countries) from 1901-2016.[10] It illustrates that average measures for this group are close to their historical peak attained subsequent to the Second World War (1941-45).[11]

Figure 1.6. **Gross general government financial liabilities of selected advanced OECD countries**

1901-2016, percentage of GDP

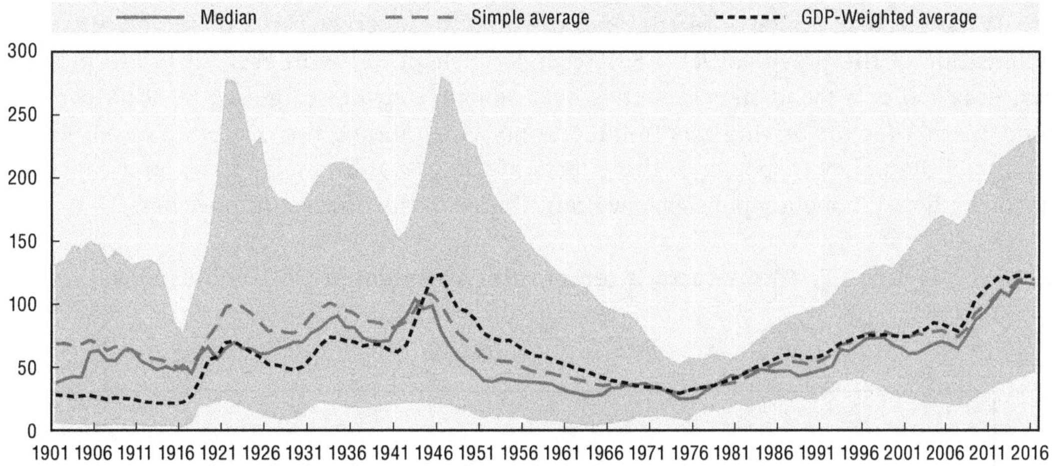

Note: The chart shows the evolution of several metrics (minimum, maximum, median, mean and GDP-weighted average) of general government gross financial liabilities expressed as a percentage of GDP for a selection of nine OECD countries (Australia, Canada, France, Germany, Italy, Japan, Spain, the United Kingdom and the United States). The grey area shows the range of minimum and maximum values all countries included. Recent data from *OECD Economic Outlook* No. 98 and earlier data estimated by extrapolating the recent data applying the dynamics observed in the gross general government debts as reported in the IMF Historical Public Debt Database. The value for Germany for the year 1925 was dropped as its low value generated an unusual volatility of debt given the pattern for Germany around that period. The remaining gaps in the time series were imputed by fitting piecewise cubic splines. Individual countries' time series may include methodological breaks. The GDP-weighted average ratio from 1954 to 2016 hinges on GDP values from IMF International Financial Statistics, converted in USD using annual exchange rates. GDP-weights before 1954 are identical to values in 1954.

Source: OECD Economic Outlook No. 98; IMF Historical Public Debt, International Financial Statistics and World Economic Outlook databases; and OECD calculations.

StatLink http://dx.doi.org/10.1787/888933393135

What is also remarkable is that the currently highest debt-to-GDP ratio of all countries included in the sample shown in Figure 1.6 is close to the two historical peaks attained after the First and the Second World War, respectively. Furthermore, the currently lowest debt-to-GDP ratio of all countries included is now well above the values observed during previous peaks (that is subsequent to the First and Second World War, respectively). This minimum is characterised by a trend increase over the last 50 years.

Taking the evidence from the various debt metrics together, public debt measures for this group of major OECD countries are currently high by historical standards. Servicing this debt is currently facilitated by low interest rates.

1.5. Interest rates are very low and sometimes even negative

Interest rates are low, by many different historical standards, both in nominal and in inflation-adjusted terms. They are low both at the short and the long end, and some rates are even negative.

The fact that interest rates are low (and some of them even negative) is the result of a variety of factors, some of which have been at play over decades. There is no consensus yet on the exact role of the various causes underlying the observed three-decade-long trend decline in interest rates, but a variety of explanations have been proposed. These include a reduction in overall global investment, perhaps related to demographic developments, and a "savings glut" in some parts of the world. Demographic developments and the role of baby boomer generations in raising the supply of savings are also often referred to in this context. Interest rates are the reflection of a variety of supply and demand factors and the interplay between them are still not very well understood.

What is clear however is that the declines in interest rates observed since the publication of the previous *OECD Sovereign Borrowing Outlook* in early 2014 are in fact a continuation of a trend that stretches over several decades (Figure 1.7). Whatever the fundamental factors driving this trend, and notwithstanding the operation of amplifying factors,[12] the policy response to the effects of the global financial crisis, and especially unconventional monetary policies, have contributed to the downward pressures.

Figure 1.7. **Short-term interest rates in selected OECD countries**

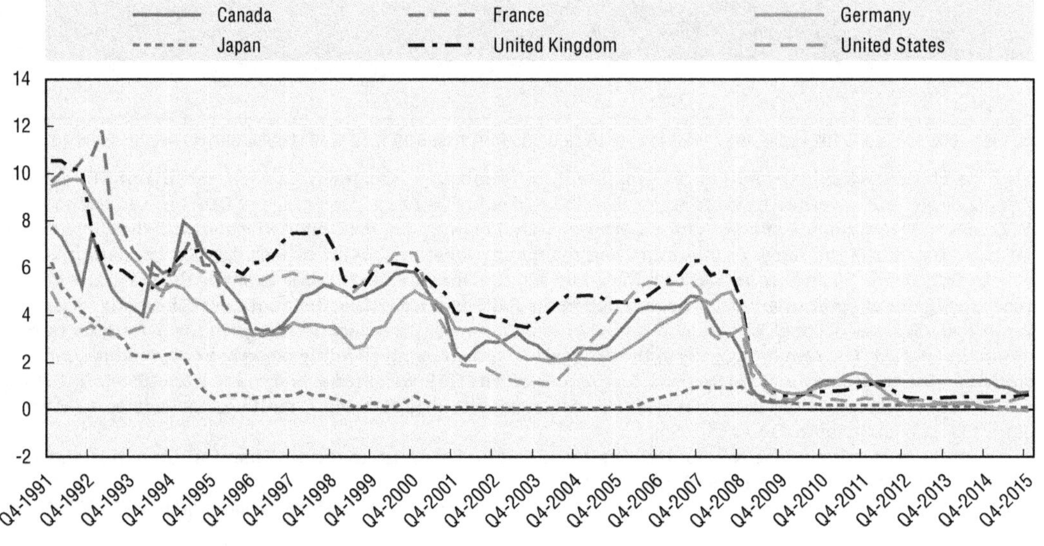

Note: Interest rates in percentages.
Source: *OECD Economic Outlook* No. 98.

StatLink http://dx.doi.org/10.1787/888933393148

In fact, several policy rates, that is interest rates at which private banks can borrow from or deposit at central banks, have been driven into negative territory. Bank deposit rates have followed in several cases. This observation is remarkable as prior to the recent episode, there was a perception among many economists and policy makers alike that nominal negative borrowing costs could not be imposed (e.g. in form of negative policy rates). The rationale for this view was that depositors would simply withdraw their money and hold cash, as long as storage costs are negligible. Recent developments cast doubt on the validity of this view, however, and/or suggest that storage costs for cash are not negligible in reality.

1.6. The medium to long-term effect of negative interest rates are not well understood yet

While so far, there have been no dramatic effects on cash demand and financial market functioning (for a recent overview see e.g. Jackson, 2015), which is reassuring, the medium- to long-run effects of negative nominal rates are not well understood yet. Concerns have been expressed that as a result of low interest rates further asset bubbles are nourished and that undesirable distributional effects are created.

Negative interest rates effectively mean that savers subsidise borrowers. Negative interest rates on sovereign bonds imply that investors compensate sovereign debtors for being able to hold their debt.

The amount of sovereign debt affected by this situation is substantial. According to BIS (2015) estimates, between December 2014 and end-May 2015, about USD 2 trillion in global long-term sovereign debt traded at negative yields on average. While rates of Treasury bonds continue to be positive and bills with shorter remaining maturities to hover close to zero in the United States, at least part of the maturity spectrum of the debt of several European sovereigns paid negative interest rates at the beginning of December 2015 (Figure 1.8). In fact, yields on the debt of some highly rated sovereigns can be negative out to more than ten years, depending on the issuer.

This interest rate environment has distributional consequences. In particular, given that governments and non-financial corporations have much larger interest-bearing liabilities than interest-earning assets, these sectors tend to benefit from ultra-low or negative interest rates. Looking at the change in net government debt interest payments, Figure 1.9 shows that many OECD countries are estimated to have benefitted from a further decline in net government debt interest payments as of GDP since the publication of the *OECD Sovereign Borrowing Outlook* 2014. Others however have not. In many cases, this situation reflects that government net debt increased, while interest rates declined.

By contrast, long-term investors such as pension funds and life insurance companies, many of which with fixed nominal payment obligations, hold more interest-bearing assets than liabilities.[13] As a result, these entities tend to suffer from lower net interest incomes in an environment of ultra-low interest rates. While some wealth effects occurred on their fixed-income portfolios as a result of declining rates over recent years, these benefits have to be seen against the background of rising measured liabilities, as lower rates to discount future payment obligations imply higher values of discounted present values of such promises. These developments have increased the already existing pressures, resulting especially from demographic developments, that a large number of financial institutions that accumulate retirement savings are facing, and it might induce them to engage in a search for yield.[14]

1.7. Interest rate expectations diverge considerably across regions

Exceptional as the current episode of low interest rates appears by historical standards, predictions of a reversal to the "normal" have so far repeatedly been proved wrong. As a result, the longer the situation of historically low rates lasts, the more observers come to believe that this situation might be the "new normal". That said, going forward, central expectations are for the situation to change and for interest rates to rise again,[15] although expected developments differ noticeably across major regions.

For example, in the euro area, market expectations are consistent with further monetary policy easing over the short term, either through additional efforts to lower short-term policy rates or long-term rates through expanded quantitative easing. Against the background of downside risks stemming especially from global growth and trade, the ECB announced that it will re-examine its monetary policy measures and use further instruments if necessary to bring inflation back to target, which is to maintain price stability and keep inflation below but close to 2% over the medium.

By contrast, in the United States, where policy rates have been lifted again for the first time in ten years in December 2015, interest rate expectations are clearly pointing

Figure 1.8. **Government benchmark interest rates in selected OECD countries**

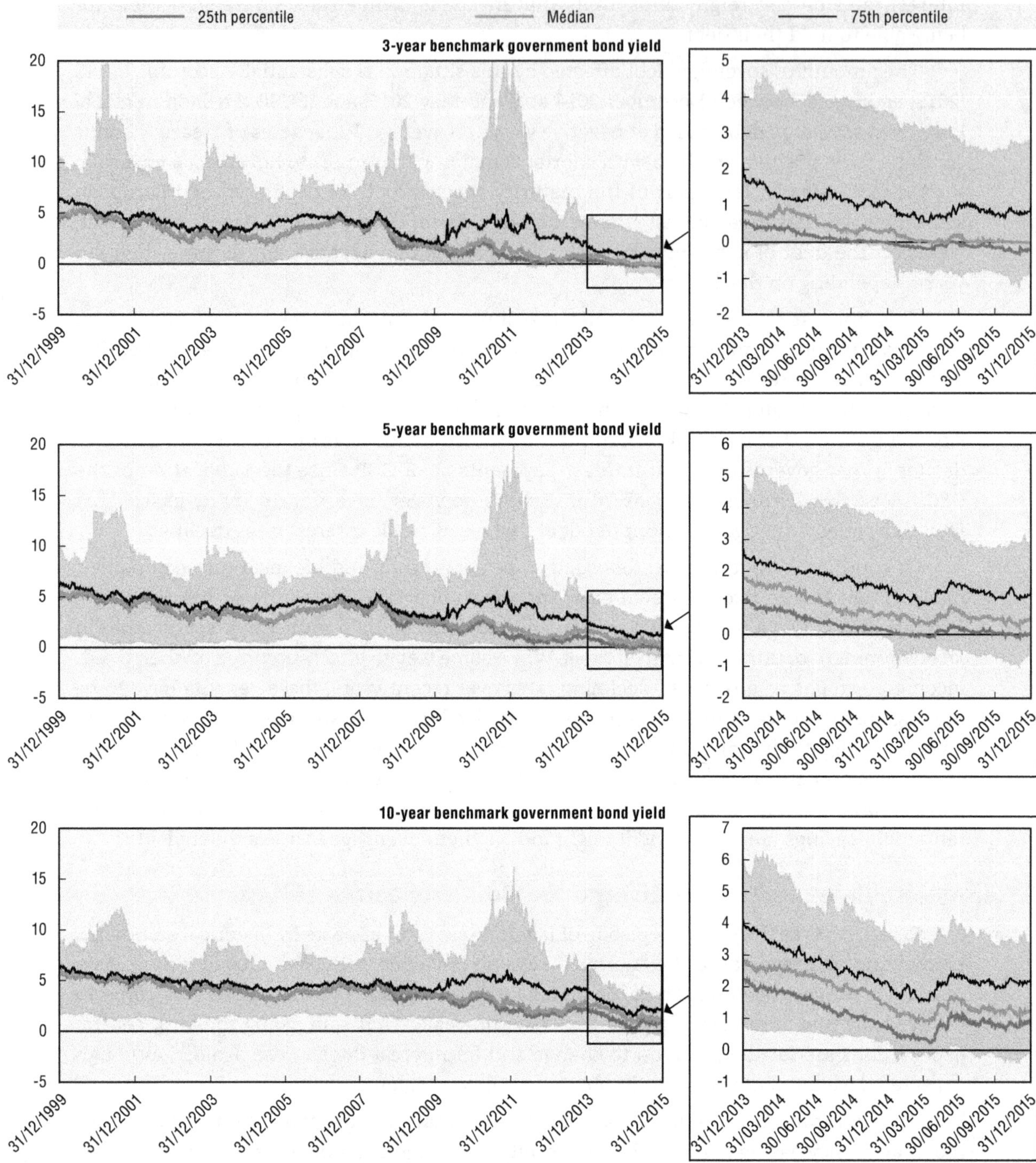

Note: Interest rates in percentages. Cut-off date is end of December 2015. The charts show the evolution of several metrics (minimum, maximum, 25th percentile, 75th percentile, median) of 3-year, 5-year and 10-year benchmark government bond yields in a group of selected OECD countries. The group includes Australia, Austria, Belgium, Canada, Denmark, Finland, France, Germany, Hungary, Ireland, Italy, Japan, Netherlands, New Zealand, Norway (5-year and 10-year yields only), Poland, Portugal, Spain, Sweden, Switzerland, United Kingdom, United States. The grey area shows the range of minimum and maximum values among all the included countries.
Source: Thomson Reuters Datastream and OECD calculations.

StatLink http://dx.doi.org/10.1787/888933393156

Figure 1.9. **Change in net government debt interest payments in selected OECD countries**

Percentage point differences

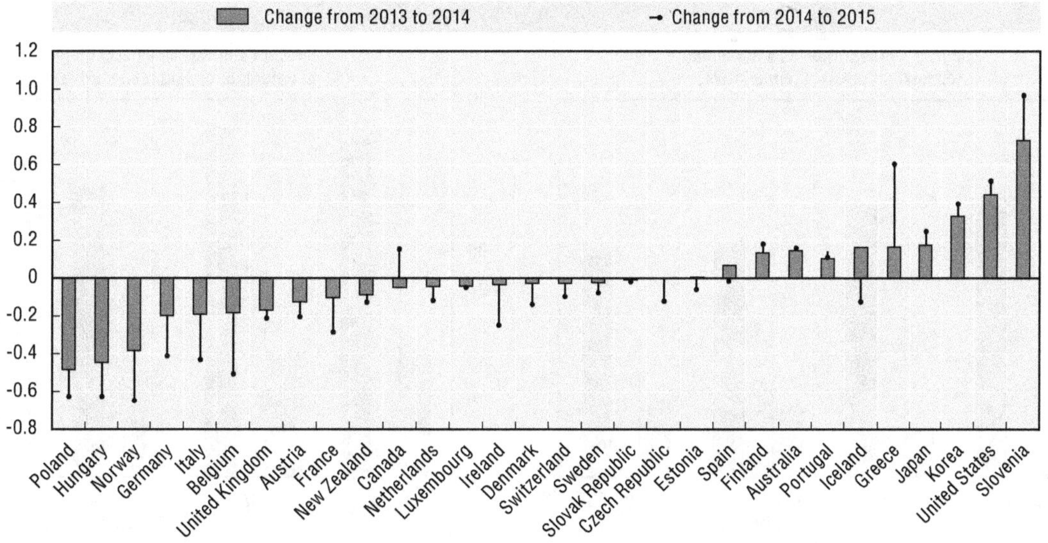

Note: Negative numbers indicate a decline in net government debt interest payments (i.e. lower net payments) as a percentage of GDP. The endpoint of the arrow indicates the change in net government debt interest payments from 2013 to 2015.

Source: OECD Economic Outlook No. 98 and OECD calculations.

StatLink http://dx.doi.org/10.1787/888933393161

upwards. There is, however, considerable uncertainty about the pace of adjustment. This uncertainty seems to have been trending up during 2015, as reflected in a relatively elevated two-year swaption volatility.[16] While short end rates volatility had been trending higher, long-end rates volatility had been trending lower during the course of the year 2015. This situation is consistent with the view that there is considerable uncertainty about the pace of United States (short-term) policy rate adjustment, while there is less uncertainty about long-term rates; the view that the latter will remain at modest levels for some time might have become more firmly entrenched.

1.8. Many debt managers are lengthening maturity profiles

The *OECD Sovereign Borrowing Outlook 2014* drew attention to the observation that many issuers faced fairly high borrowing needs and challenging redemption profiles at least until 2017. The observation is still valid. While gross and net borrowing needs have somewhat decreased since the publication of the 2014 edition, redemption profiles continue to be challenging, with more than a third of total outstanding long-term debt and close to 45% of total debt in 2015 estimated to be coming due over the three years from 2015 to 2018 (Figure 1.10).

This situation places a premium on management of debt maturities to control rollover risk. The responses of debt management offices to this situation and the choices made as part of their funding strategy in primary and secondary markets are discussed in more detail in the remaining chapters of this Sovereign Borrowing Outlook. The remainder of this section singles out for special attention some observations regarding developments in the maturity structure of issuance and outstanding debt.

Figure 1.10. **Cumulative percentage of debt maturing in the next 12, 24 and 36 months**

As a percentage of total marketable debt as of 2015

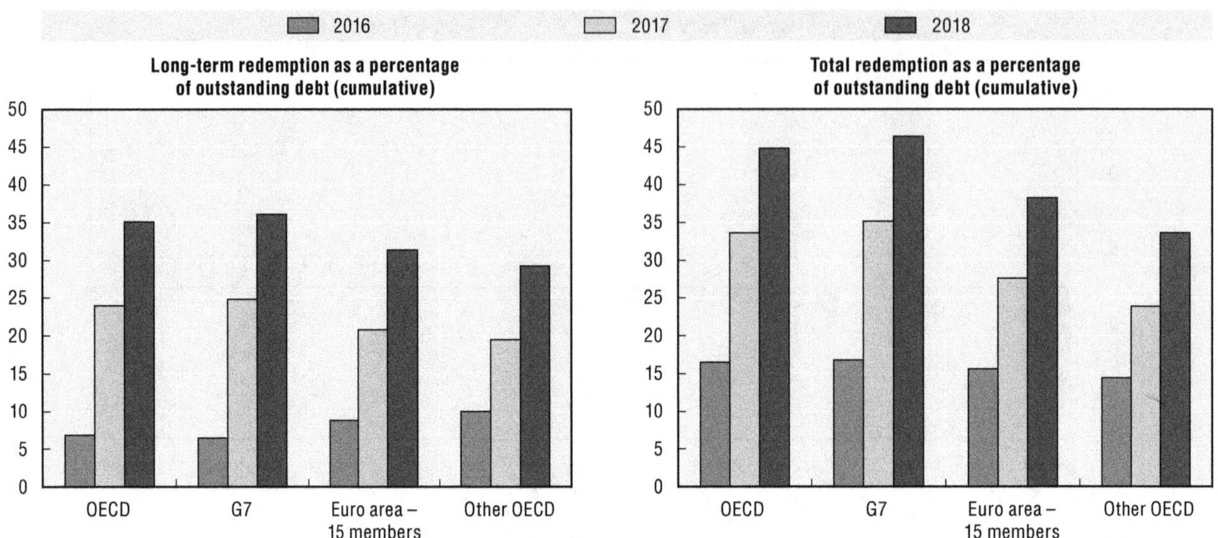

Note: Cumulative percentage of debt maturing in the next 12, 24 and 36 months (i.e. in 2016, 2017 and 2018, respectively) as a percentage of total marketable debt stock (without cash) in 2015. Values of principal payments and marketable debt have been aggregated into a single currency by using fixed exchange rates, as of 1 December 2009, for all years. The euro area – 15 members – include Austria, Belgium, Estonia, Finland, France, Germany, Greece, Ireland, Italy, Luxembourg, Netherlands, Portugal, Slovak Republic, Slovenia and Spain. "Other OECD" countries include Australia, Chile, Czech Republic, Denmark, Hungary, Iceland, Israel, Mexico, New Zealand, Norway, Poland, Sweden, Switzerland and Turkey. Korea is not included in the chart.

Source: 2015 Survey on central government marketable debt and borrowing by the OECD Working Party on Debt Management; Bloomberg; and OECD calculations.

StatLink http://dx.doi.org/10.1787/888933393046

In describing the maturity structure of debt and communicating about roll-over risks, debt management offices often refer to traditional and conceptually straightforward sovereign debt metrics such as the average or weighted-average maturity of debt outstanding. With an average maturity of four years, the total debt is rolled over once every four years. If the average debt maturity was increased from four to five years, only 20% instead of 25% of debt would mature each year and would thus have to be refunded, assuming net borrowing requirements equal to zero.

A lengthening of the maturity structure of government debt can be a cost-minimising response to a highly uncertain future issuance environment. On the one hand, extending the average maturity of debt implies that roll-over risk is reduced. On the other, as yield curves are typically upward-sloping, such strategies involve higher measured debt-servicing costs over the short term. Currently, the term premium seems to have become smaller than it used to be in the past. Thus, the trade-off between expected higher cost associated with a longer duration and reduced roll-over risk is changing, with the result that it becomes relatively cheaper to limit roll-over risk. Longer durations imply that borrowing costs become more predictable over time and this advantage might be achieved currently at more limited costs than in the past.

In fact, the maturity structure of gross issuance of central government marketable debt has evolved over recent years and is characterized by a trend increase in the issuance of long-term as opposed to short-term debt instruments in the area as a whole (Figure 1.11). As a result of this trend in issuance, the structure of outstanding debt is also changing. While the

Figure 1.11. **Maturity structure of gross issuance operations in the OECD area**

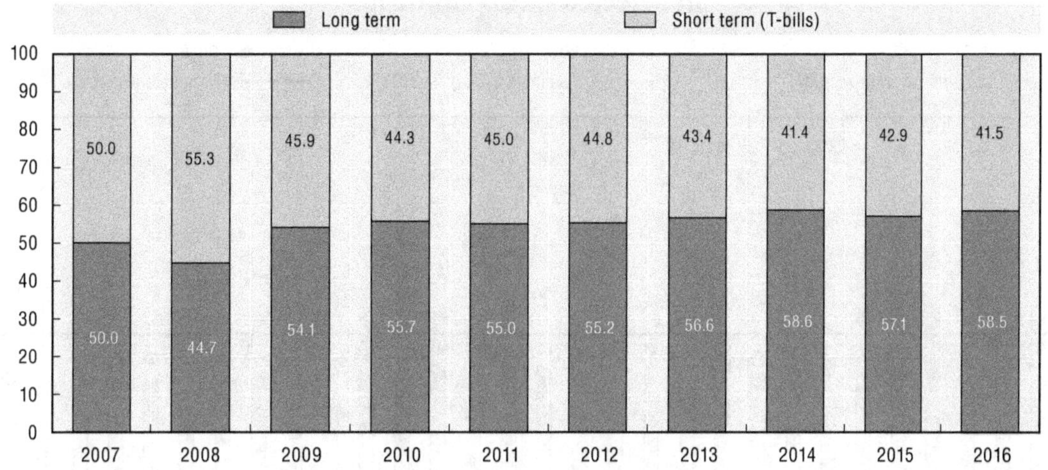

Long term | Short term (T-bills)

2007: 50.0 / 50.0
2008: 44.7 / 55.3
2009: 54.1 / 45.9
2010: 55.7 / 44.3
2011: 55.0 / 45.0
2012: 55.2 / 44.8
2013: 56.6 / 43.4
2014: 58.6 / 41.4
2015: 57.1 / 42.9
2016: 58.5 / 41.5

Source: 2015 Survey on central government marketable debt and borrowing by the OECD Working Party on Debt Management; Bloomberg, national authorities' websites and OECD calculations.

StatLink http://dx.doi.org/10.1787/888933393053

response to the financial crisis involved a sharp increase in the share of short-term central government marketable debt of almost 4% to around 18% from 2008 to 2009, this share is estimated to have substantially fallen again. It is estimated to be below 10% of total outstanding central government marketable debt in the OECD area as a whole in 2015, thus well below the levels observed between 2007 and 2009 (Figure 1.12).

Figure 1.12. **Maturity structure of central government marketable debt for OECD area**

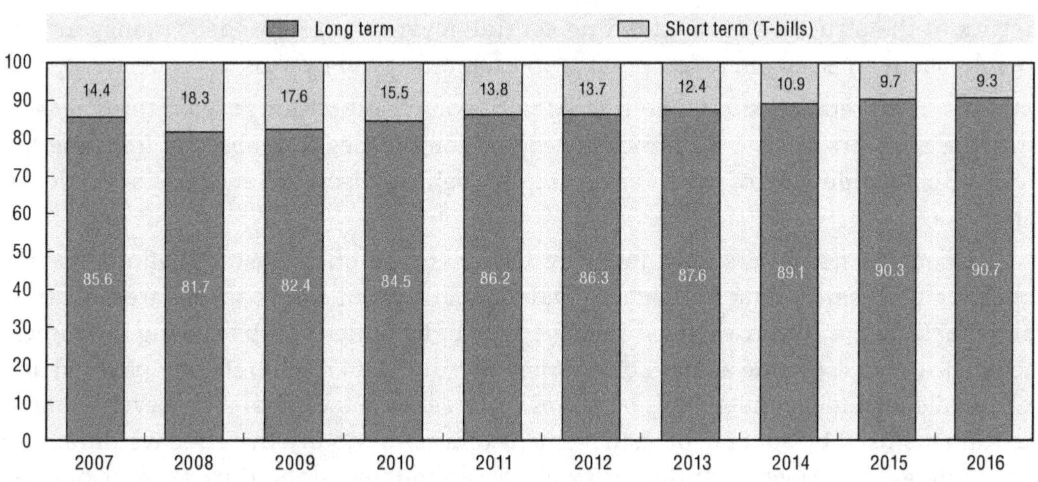

Source: 2015 Survey on central government marketable debt and borrowing by the OECD Working Party on Debt Management; Bloomberg, national authorities' websites and OECD calculations.

StatLink http://dx.doi.org/10.1787/888933393067

This change in the structure of outstanding debt is consistent with a lengthening of the maturity of debt and, in fact, the average maturity of outstanding marketable central government debt in selected OECD countries has continued to increase over recent years. It is estimated to be close to eight years in 2015, compared to just above seven years in 2013 (Figure 1.13). In 2007, this measure stood at 6.5 years. Thus, judged by this simple standard

Figure 1.13. **Average term-to-maturity of outstanding marketable debt in selected OECD countries**

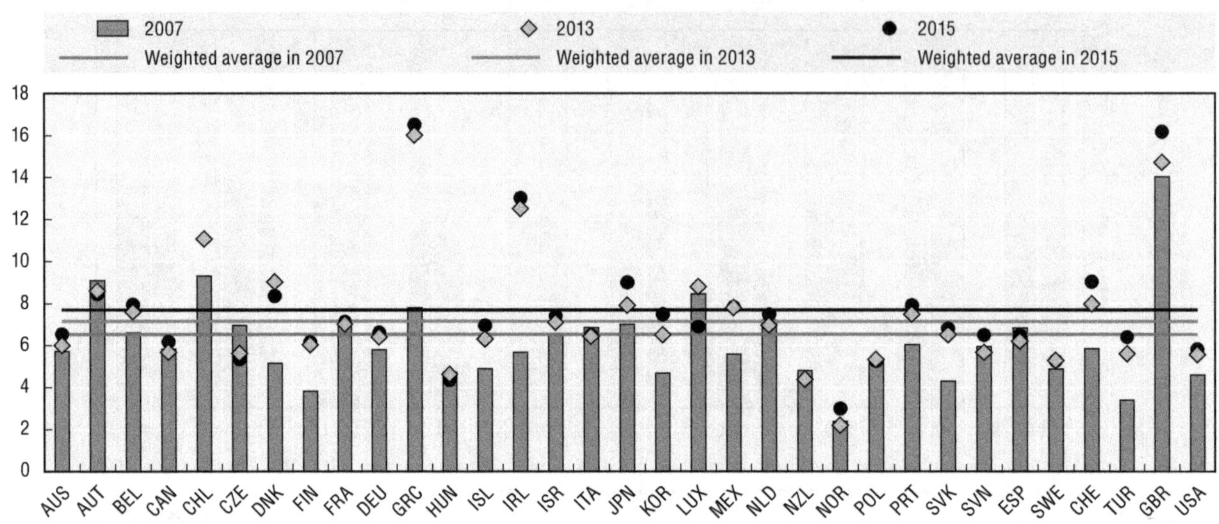

Note: Average term-to-maturity in years (e.g. 0.5 years correspond to 6 months) of outstanding marketable debt. Data are collected from debt management office and national authorities' websites. Data are not strictly comparable across countries. The average term-to-maturity of outstanding debt might include government holdings (e.g. Norway, the United Kingdom), might include short-term debt (e.g. Denmark, United Kingdom) or exclude it (e.g. Ireland), include the effect of swaps (e.g. for France and Norway) or exclude that effect. The weighted average was calculated based on the data of all countries for which the average term to maturity was available for 2007, 2013, and 2015. The values of central government marketable debt (without cash) in 2007, 2013 and 2015, expressed in USD values using the December 2009 exchange rates, were used as weights in constructing the average. Figures for 2015 refer to the latest, publicly available, information. Cut-off date is 11 December 2015.

Source: Surveys on central government marketable debt and borrowing by the OECD Working Party on Debt Management; debt management offices and national authorities' websites and OECD calculations.

StatLink http://dx.doi.org/10.1787/888933393078

metrics of the structure of outstanding central government debt, debt managers have brought about an easing in redemption profiles, limiting roll-over risk.

This interpretation should be treated with some caution for at least three reasons. First, the numbers refer to a metrics of redemption profiles that abstract from the total levels of outstanding debt, which are currently high, as discussed in the first sections of this chapter.

Second, the numbers shown in Figure 1.13 are based on consistent definitions when collecting time-series data for each individual country, but the concepts are not strictly comparable across countries given that the type of liabilities and borrowing instruments included are not the same across border. Moreover, the data might refer to "physical debt" only, while excluding the effects of swaps. Interest rate swaps are, however, standard instruments used by some debt management offices to modify the effective duration of outstanding debt. Most recently, for example, a strategy adopted by at least one debt management office consists of extending the duration of debt in small steps by limiting the use of swaps, which are being used to effectively lower the duration of debt given the duration of outstanding government bonds.

Third, using average debt maturity as a metrics to describe redemption profiles has well-known limits. Against the background of this observation, dent management offices are developing and monitoring a host of other indicators to assess roll-over risks as well as to communicate debt management strategies. Some metrics are based on surveys of primary dealers and investors and others involve fairly complex methods, involving stochastic simulations. As a gauge of roll-over risk, average debt maturity is deficient in capturing a variety of issues such as the frequency of required or planned market access and potential redemption cliffs, i.e. situations where redemptions are not smoothly distributed over time. More generally, just like any average measure, average-debt-to-maturity does not provide information about the distribution of redemptions over time of existing sovereign debt portfolios.

Some of the more recent sovereign debt metrics use stochastic simulations to describe the issuance strategy (i.e. issuance size and distribution over different maturities, etc.) as a function of the projected economic and financial markets environment (projected interest rates and budget deficits, etc.). To what extent such alternative metrics should be used in the communication with potential investors, so as to add quantitative references to qualitative announcements, is one of the many issues currently being discussed among debt management offices. Discussions within the OECD Working Party on Debt Management suggest that a consensus has yet to be reached regarding the pros and cons of using more sophisticated and perhaps more difficult-to-explain metrics as part of public communication in an effort to further enhance transparency of debt management strategies. In any case, such more sophisticated debt metrics allow debt managers to place a sharp focus on limiting tail outcomes by using quantitative tools that capture the likelihood of their occurrence under different borrowing strategy choices. Avoiding such risks is crucial, as debt managers have a natural inclination to prepare for the worst. The fulfilment of their mandates typically does benefit more from avoiding downside risks than exploiting upside risks.

1.9. Other aspects of funding strategies in terms of types of instruments

The funding strategy of debt management offices is guided primarily by considerations regarding the costs and risks of the management of debt. The mandates of debt managers typically have a clear microeconomic focus, involving attempts to keep sovereign debt markets liquid and limit refunding risks, etc., while references to macroeconomic objectives in formal mandates are rare and/or formulated in terms of ensuring broad consistency with macroeconomic policy objectives. Nonetheless, debt management does not operate in a vacuum, and funding strategy choices take this observation into account.

The funding strategy entails decisions on how gross borrowing needs are funded using instruments with different maturities and other features. Table 1.2 reflects the choices

Table 1.2. **Funding strategy based on marketable gross borrowing needs in OECD area**

Percentage

	2007	2008	2009	2010	2011	2012	2013	2014	2015	2016
Short Term (T-bills)	**50.0**	**55.3**	**45.9**	**44.3**	**45.0**	**44.8**	**43.4**	**41.4**	**42.9**	**41.5**
Long Term	**50.0**	**44.7**	**54.1**	**55.7**	**55.0**	**55.2**	**56.6**	**58.6**	**57.1**	**58.5**
Fixed rate	43.8	40.0	50.1	51.4	50.4	51.0	51.1	51.6	50.3	51.5
Index linked	3.3	2.5	1.8	2.3	3.0	3.2	3.7	4.1	3.9	4.0
Variable rate	1.6	1.0	1.0	0.9	0.7	0.3	0.9	2.4	2.4	2.4
Other	1.3	1.1	1.2	1.1	0.9	0.7	0.7	0.6	0.5	0.5
Of which:										
Local currency	49.7	44.1	53.4	55.3	54.6	55.3	55.9	57.8	56.5	57.9
Foreign currency	0.3	0.5	0.7	0.5	0.4	0.5	0.6	0.7	0.5	0.6

Source: 2015 Survey on central government marketable debt and borrowing by the OECD Working Party on Debt Management; Bloomberg, national authorities' websites and OECD calculations.

StatLink http://dx.doi.org/10.1787/888933393249

made regarding the funding structure in terms of types of instruments and maturity. The relative importance of issuance of short-term instruments was relatively high in 2008 and 2007, but has lessened since then. Currently, around 55% of funding of gross borrowing needs is covered by long-term instruments, dominated by fixed rate, local currency bonds. The issuance of index-linked bonds is estimated to have increased to above pre-crisis levels, and remain at those more elevated levels during the projection period. Variable-rate debt has increased noticeably. Also, somewhat more foreign-currency debt was issued in 2014 and this funding pattern is estimated to broadly remain at that slightly more elevated level. More details of funding patterns are provided in the chapters on challenges in primary and secondary markets of this *Outlook*.

1.10. Monetary policy and debt management decisions influence each other

As has been noted, as a response to the global financial crisis and deteriorating real activity outlook, central banks in the major advanced economies lowered policy rates to close to zero, or even below, and several of them also implemented policy measures considered unconventional, including outright purchases of large amounts of long-term bonds. Such measures were aimed at affecting real activity through several channels, including through the portfolio balance channel, whereby purchases of longer-term securities lower the long end of the yield curve and lead investors to buy assets with even greater duration or higher credit risk.[17] Examples of quantitative easing strategies that have had a direct impact on sovereign debt markets include the Federal Reserve's Large-Scale Asset Purchase (LSAP) Programme introduced in 2008, the Maturity Extension Programme (MEP) of 2011 and the ECB's Outright Monetary Transactions (OMT) Programme. More recently, in January 2015, the ECB announced the asset purchase programme (APP), which has the objective to provide additional monetary policy stimulus in face of increasing deflation risks and to ease borrowing conditions of households and firms. Many of these policies led to a massive expansion of the balance sheets of central banks (Figure 1.9).[18]

There is considerable scope for consultation between central banks and sovereign debt managers, especially as their respective mandates imply that they operate in the same markets. That said, parts of the mandates of central banks and debt managers are at odds, which is why perfect collaboration is not feasible and perhaps not even desirable. The observation that potential tensions could arise justifies however close communication. In fact, central banks and debt managers are operating in the same markets and, thus, effective two-way exchange of information between the government debt issuers and the central bank is important, not least to avoid the impression on the part of other market participants that their respective strategies are at odds and could create additional frictions.

Debt management aims at matching government borrowing needs at the lowest costs while maintaining risk at acceptable levels. Achieving this mandate can involve shortening or lengthening the maturity structure of government debt. If the maturity structure of the debt is shortened, the debt instruments represent more liquidity for their holders, which likely influences spending. By contrast, if the maturity structure is lengthened, the effects on spending plans will be in the opposite direction. When central banks implemented quantitative easing measures over recent years with the aim of lowering long-term sovereign bond rates and encouraging additional risk-taking, public debt management strategies that involved extended average maturity of debt to lock in low long-term rates tended to countervail the desired long-term-rate reduction effects. For example, according to Meaning and Zhu (2012), the US Treasury's extension of average maturity of outstanding debt, by around twelve months between 2009 and 2011 pushed 10-year benchmark bond rates up by several tens of basis points. The authors conclude that while unconventional monetary policy was effective in lowering long-term government bond yields, the impact of bond purchases on the 10-year bond yield would have been greater had the Treasury not expanded the relative supply of Treasuries at the long end, thus increasing the average maturity of outstanding Treasury debt. Debt management offices are aware of these potential tensions and address them by adopting transparent and predictable issuance strategies.

Similarly, transparency and communication on the part of the central bank is important to ensure that an unwinding of unconventional policy measures and government bond sales by central banks are not disruptive for markets. Central banks are aware of the implications for sovereign debt markets of an exit from quantitative easing and do in fact communicate to the public their intentions so as to limit uncertainty. For example, the Bank of England Monetary Policy Council (MPC), which decided to give preference to adjusting policy through using the Bank Rate rather than the stock of assets purchased, announced that it expects to continue to reinvest maturing assets until the Bank Rate has reached a level from which it can again be cut materially (Bank of England, 2015). Moreover, the MPC suggests "any reduction in the stock of purchased assets will be conducted in an orderly manner over a period of time so as not to disrupt the gilt market. So, while any reduction will be solely a decision for the MPC based on meeting its objectives, the Bank will liaise with the Debt Management Office when implementing any change in its asset purchase programme." Similarly, as part of the press conference related to the December Federal Open Market Committee meeting in December 2015, the Fed Chair emphasized that tapering reinvestment will be delayed until after policy rate normalization is "well under way." This communication is consistent with a desire to return to an interest rate level from which rates could be cut again in the case of a negative shock before starting to run down the central bank balance sheet.

1.11. The role of public institutions as investors in sovereign bonds has risen

The role of public sector institutions, including but not limited to central banks, as investors in sovereign bonds has increased during the last decade. The quantitative easing programs have been reflected in a marked increase in the significance of central banks as sovereign bond investors over recent years, while the substantial accumulation of foreign exchange reserves especially of many emerging markets for more than a decade has implied a more gradual increase in public sector holdings of sovereign debt. Other public sector institutions such as sovereign wealth funds have also taken on greater significance as investors. The various types of public sector investors, including central banks and sovereign wealth funds, that have increased their demand for high-quality sovereign debt issues do not form a homogeneous group, although there are some common issues that their increased participation as investors raises.

One issue that the increased participation of public institutions as investors raises is that to the extent that they are large, holdings of sovereign bonds might become more concentrated. This situation in turn could have adverse effects on bond market volatility, as even relatively small reallocations and portfolio adjustments on the part of such large investors could have significant price implications. For example, the role of foreign central banks matters in the case of the market for US government debt. Towards the end of 2015, some of the latter were selling US Treasuries, which could have had noticeable price implications had these sales not been more than offset by foreign private buyers. In fact, in this specific case, a decline in official holdings put upward pressure on rates, but the interest from private investors, presumably motivated by the stronger real activity outlook in the United States compared to some other regions, seem to have capped secondary market yield increases.

Figure 1.14. **Total balance sheets of selected central banks**

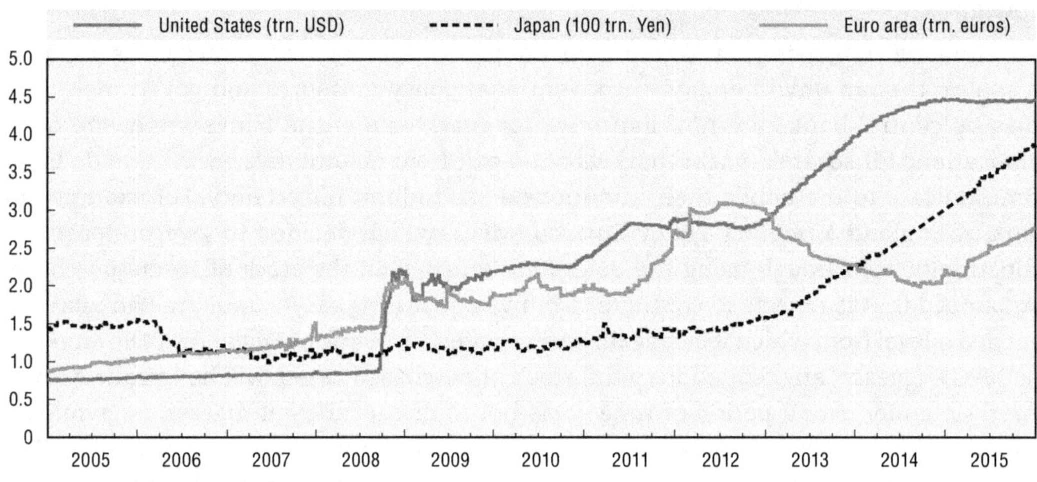

Note: Cutoff date is end of December 2015.
Source: Thomson Reuters Datastream.

StatLink http://dx.doi.org/10.1787/888933393088

Another issue is related to market liquidity. Many of the public institutions that have assumed a greater role as investors in sovereign bonds apply buy-and-hold strategies, implying that the increased participation of such investors might in principle decrease bond market liquidity. Against the background of the potential issue of such a situation, international best-practise guidelines for debt managers recommend having a diversified investor base. That said, there is no generally accepted specific definition of what defines such an investor base. Debt managers recognise, however, that it is most desirable to achieve a well-balanced mix of investors with different mandates and investment horizons, and debt managers currently focus on bringing in new investors from diverse backgrounds.

1.12. The issue of liquidity and liquidity risk has come into sharp focus

The issue of bond market liquidity and liquidity risk has come into a sharp spotlight, among other things reflecting recent experiences with episodes of exceptional high volatility in specific market segments, including in those for securities that are traditionally characterised by high liquidity. One type of concern regarding market liquidity is related to the question of what happens when interest rates might rise by more than factored into current prices.

Many asset prices including those for corporate bonds in emerging markets rose significantly over the past five years or so; they were supported by low interest rates, but remain vulnerable to sharper-than-expected increases in interest rates. The effects on these and other asset prices could be magnified by sudden disappearances in market liquidity (BoE, 2015b).

Concerns are not limited to markets for emerging and advanced economies corporate bond markets. In fact, secondary bond market liquidity is a concern across different types of markets, and sovereign bond markets are no exception.

The issue of liquidity or the lack of it is an especially important issue in the case of government bond markets, given their crucial economic function. These markets serve to fund the governments' borrowing needs and support the conduct of monetary policy. Government bonds are used as collateral in various transactions conducted bilaterally and through clearing houses and exchanges. They are a global reserve asset and their prices are used by market participants to price other assets and manage interest-rate risk. As a result of these various functions of government bonds, liquidity in the markets in these assets is of great importance.

Debt managers have expressed concerns about secondary market liquidity and liquidity risk in securities markets including sovereign bond markets. Some observers have argued that market making has become more costly as a result of financial regulatory reform, although such a direct link has been difficult to prove (CGFS, 2014). Other observers point to a host of other potential determinants of liquidity, including market participants' risk appetites and changing technologies.

Measuring liquidity is not straightforward and there is no single measure of market liquidity capturing the various dimensions of this concept. And whether pre-crisis levels are a good reference is questionable. In any case, the issue is not so much liquidity *per se* but liquidity risk, that is, the risk that liquidity suddenly disappears. The factors behind the evolution of liquidity and especially liquidity risk are not yet well understood, however, and more research is needed.

Liquidity and liquidity risk in any market segment are influenced by the constraints facing and the behaviour of various actors active on the demand or supply side of a specific market segment. Debt management offices are addressing the issue of liquidity risk among other things by stepping up their effects to monitor liquidity indicators, and they also put in place several measures to better evaluate and motivate dealer performance in market-making, as well as adapted their own issuance strategies. The latter has involved buying back illiquid lines, strengthening existing benchmark lines and increasing transparency through a variety of measures. More detail is provided in the subsequent chapters that discuss developments in primary and secondary market liquidity and liquidity risks based on a survey among debt management offices that are members of the OECD Working Party on Debt Management.

Debt management offices express considerable concern regarding secondary sovereign bond market liquidity, especially in the case of bonds that are not "on-the run". These concerns are valid, although it is useful to recall that there is no wide-spread agreement on how to measure market liquidity. This situation reflects not only the observation that market liquidity has many dimensions; that is, a market is considered liquid when sizeable quantities can be negotiated quickly and at a price close to the market price. It also reflects the observation that the various dimensions, e.g. size and speed, are not equally valuable in all situations, that is whether market conditions are normal or stressed.

While most traditional and many more modern liquidity indicators do not clearly signal a decline in liquidity during normal times, the incidence of episodes where liquidity suddenly dries up in stress situations without any clear economic justifications might have become more numerous, including especially in the case of benchmark securities that are otherwise regarded as being highly liquid (Powell, 2015). As concerns about secondary market liquidity are valid, more research is needed to more fully understand the implications of the evolving sovereign bond market structures and the effect of structural changes and regulation for liquidity, trading and risk management practices, and market monitoring.

Notes

1. The cut-off date for data collected through the Survey on central government marketable debt and borrowing by the OECD Working Party on Debt Management is mid-November 2015 and the cut-off date for other data considered in this chapter is 31 December 2015.
2. See Table 1.4 of *OECD Economic Outlook*, Volume 2015, Issue 2.
3. This assessment is based on estimates of OECD aggregates using the assumption of exchange rates that are fixed as of 1 December 2009 when converting national values to USD equivalents. Accounting for exchange rate developments (annual period-average exchange rates, with rates kept constant after cut-off date 1 December 2015), estimates of net central government marketable borrowing requirements for 2016 are USD 500 billion (rather than USD 600 billion, as reported above).
4. The OECD *Sovereign Borrowing Outlook* 2014 expected combined gross borrowing needs of OECD countries to fall from USD 11 trillion in 2012 to USD 10.8 trillion in 2013 and further to USD 10.6 trillion in 2014, again based on the assumption of fixed exchange rates in the aggregation process. Using that same assumption and recent information, central government gross borrowing requirements for 2012 to 2014 were USD 10.7, 10.4, and 10.1 trillion, respectively, and are estimated to further decline to USD 9.4 trillion in 2015 and USD 8.8 trillion in 2016.
5. Redemptions include those of long-term and short-term debt. As regards the latter, the method for calculating gross short-term borrowing needs suggested in Annex B.6 of the *Sovereign Borrowing Outlook* 2014 is followed here.
6. Using flexible rather than fixed exchange rate assumptions to obtain area-wide data from national data, the estimated decline would be from USD 9.7 trillion in 2013 to USD 8.0 in 2015. As in the case of net borrowing requirements, the difference in estimates of gross borrowing requirements as a result of the choice of exchange rate assumption owes much to the observed depreciation of the Japanese Yen versus the USD over recent years. Using more up-to-date exchange rate assumptions imply a lower "weight" in OECD aggregates of Japanese borrowing metrics.
7. Reflecting the effect of the observed Yen-versus-USD depreciation, forward-looking assessments depend to some extent on the choice of exchange rate assumption when aggregating national date. The *OECD Sovereign Borrowing Outlook* has traditionally relied on the assumption of exchange rates fixed as of 2009. If one considers flexible exchange rates, debt would be estimated to decline from 2014 to 2015 and then to rise from 2015 to 2016, although not exceeding in 2016 the level attained in 2014.
8. The global financial crisis placed a sharp spotlight not only on levels of actual public debt but also on the issue of contingent sovereign liabilities, especially those stemming from banking sector liabilities. In fact, the global financial crisis that initially started out as a crisis involving private financial intermediaries evolved into a sovereign debt crisis with the focal point in Europe, among other things as a result of adverse feedback loops operating between sovereign and banking sector debt in some economies. A variety of fiscal and regulatory measures were invoked to break that adverse feedback loop. Among these, the strengthening of banking sector regulation and of capital and liquidity buffers in that sector have been successful in limiting undesirable adverse feedback loops. Banks'capital and liquidity buffers are being strengthened, while the burden of potential failure resolution needs is shifted from the taxpayer to bank creditors. As a result, implicit contingent liabilities stemming from efforts to avoid or deal with banking sector failures have declined (Cariboni et al., 2016; Blix-Grimaldi et al., 2016; Arslanalp and Liao, 2015). Admittedly, public authorities have not yet settled on the best way of measuring such liabilities (Schich and Aydin, 2014), but the observation that the results of several different approaches point in a similar direction is reassuring.
9. Some caution is required in interpreting these ratios as both numerator and denominator for these two years are based on estimates/projections.
10. Note that this reference is to general as opposed to central government debt, unlike the preceding discussion. An excellent overview of different government debt indicators is provided by Bloch and Fall (2015).

11. These measures are constructed by combining a time series for general government gross financial liabilities as a percentage of GDP from the OECD and the IMF. To facilitate updating most recent estimates, the general approach taken was to consider OECD data for the recent history and going back in time as far as appeared reasonable and then to extrapolate the data by applying the changes observed in the IMF data (which goes further back in time). As there are some level differences between OECD and IMF data (with the former tending to exceed the latter), the estimates of the peaks attained subsequent to World War II using the method underlying the data shown in the figure are higher than what IMF data would have suggested.
12. Domanski, Shin and Sushkoportfolio (2015) analyse how adjustments by long-term investors aimed at containing duration mismatches have acted as an amplification mechanism in the process of interest rate compression.
13. Similarly, the household sector has more interest-bearing assets than interest-bearing liabilities, which is why that sector's net interest income tends to be adversely affected by a low-interest-rate environment. At the same time, households benefit from capital gains on fixed-income asset holdings, although such holdings are not equally distributed within the household sector. A recent study, focusing directly on the effects of unconventional monetary policy measures in Japan, argues that increases in financial asset prices while the overall real economy was stagnant has disproportionally benefitted higher-income households, which tend to hold greater amounts of financial assets than low-income households. See Saiki and Frost (2014).
14. On the challenges for pension funds and life insurance companies in a situation of protracted low interest rates see *OECD Business and Finance Outlook* (2015), *OECD Pension Market in Focus* (2015) and Antolin, Schich and Yermo (2011).
15. This assessment is consistent with forward interest rates, although the situation differs noticeably across regions. There are some observations that suggest that some of the savings supply factors are evolving (Bean et al., 2015). For example, aggregate savings propensities should fall back as the bulge of high-saving middle-aged households moves through into retirement and start to dissave; this process has already begun. Also, the net flow of Chinese savings into global financial markets has already started to ebb.
16. A swaption is an option granting its owner the right (but not the obligation) to enter into an underlying swap, often (as is the case here) referring to interest rate swaps. In such a transaction, typically, two counterparties agree to exchange a stream of cash flows over some specified period of time, with one counterparty receiving a fixed payment stream and paying the other party a stream of floating cash flows tied to the three-month Libor rate. A swap can be interpreted as trading a fixed rate coupon bond for a floating rate note.
17. Also, to the extent that the signalling via asset purchases of the commitment to further stimulus going forward is credible, a lower expected path of short-term rates will result, with reduced long-term rates and compressed risk premia due to the reduction in uncertainty.
18. Unlike the Large-Scale Asset Purchase Programme, the Maturity Extension Programme aims at extending the average maturity of the Treasury securities held by the Federal Reserve, while holding the overall size of the central bank's balance sheet constant. Empirical analyses of the effects of the various programmes suggest that the effects on assets targeted were generally found to be significant, although declining over time and often with limited spill-overs to other market segments. In the UK, however, there is evidence that scarcity effects on the targeted maturities of gilts have spilled over to other asset classes of similar maturity; see McLaren et al. (2014).

References

Arslanalp, S. and Y. Liao (2015), "Contingent Liabilities from Banks: How to Track Them?", *IMF Working Paper* WP/15/255, December, *www.imf.org/external/pubs/ft/wp/2015/wp15255.pdf*.

Altavilla, C., G. Carboni and R. Motto (2015), "Asset purchase programmes and financial markets: lessons from the euro area", *ECB Working Paper* No. 1864, November, *www.ecb.europa.eu/pub/pdf/scpwps/ecbwp1864.en.pdf?9f482224ba19759047b2c7f85670b0d3*.

Antolin, P., Sebastian Schich and Juan Yermo (2011), "The Economic Impact of Protracted Low Interest Rates on Pension Funds and Insurance Companies", *OECD Journal: Financial Market Trends*, Vol. 2011/1, *http://dx.doi.org/10.1787/fmt-2011-5kg55qw0m56l*.

Bean C., C. Broda, T. Ito and R. Kroszner (2015), "Low for Long? Causes and Consequences of Persistently Low Interest Rates", The 17th Geneva Report on the World Economy, CEPR, London, 23 October, *www.voxeu.org/content/low-long-causes-and-consequences-persistently-low-interest-rates*.

Bank of England (2015), *Inflation Report*, November 2015, *www.bankofengland.co.uk/publications/Pages/inflationreport/2015/nov.aspx*.

Bank of England (2015b), *Financial Stability Report*, Issue No. 38, December 2015, *www.bankofengland.co.uk/publications/Documents/fsr/2015/dec.pdf*.

BIS (2015), "Is the unthinkable becoming routine?", Chapter 1 of 85th *Annual Report* 2014/15, 28 June 2015, *www.bis.org/publ/arpdf/ar2015e1.htm*.

Blix-Grimaldi, M., J. Hofmeister, S. Schich and D. Snethlage (2016), "Estimating the size and incidence of bank resolution costs for selected banks in OECD countries", OECD *Financial Market Trends*, Volume 2016-Issue 1 (forthcoming).

Bloch, D. and F. Fall (2015), "Government debt indicators: Understanding the data", *OECD Economics Department Working Papers*, No. 1228, OECD Publishing, Paris, *http://dx.doi.org/10.1787/5jrxv0ftbff2-en*.

Blommestein, H.J. and P. Turner (2012), "Interactions Between Sovereign Debt Management and Monetary Policy Under Fiscal Dominance and Financial Instability", *OECD Working Papers on Sovereign Borrowing and Public Debt Management*, No. 3, OECD Publishing, Paris, *http://dx.doi.org/10.1787/5k9fdwrnd1g3-en*.

Cariboni, J., A. Fontana, S. Langedijk, S. Maccaferri, A. Pagano, M. Petracco Giudici, M. Rancan, and S. Schich (2016), "Reducing and sharing the burden of bank failures", OECD *Financial Market Trends*, Volume 2016-Issue 1 (forthcoming).

Committee on the Global Financial System (CGFS, 2014), "Market-making and proprietary trading: Industry trends, drivers and policy implications", *CGFS Paper* No. 52, November 2014, *www.bis.org/publ/cgfs52.htm*.

Jackson, H. (2015), "The International Experience with Negative Policy Rates", Bank of Canada, *Staff Discussion Paper* 2015-13, November, *www.bankofcanada.ca/2015/11/staff-discussion-paper-2015-13/*.

McLaren, N., R.N. Banerjee and D. Latto (2014), "Using changes in Auction Maturity Sectors to help identify the impact of QE on Gilt Yields", *The Economic Journal*, Vol. 124(576), 453-479, *http://onlinelibrary.wiley.com/doi/10.1111/ecoj.12141/abstract*.

Meaning, J. and F. Zhu (2012), "The impact of Federal Reserve asset purchase programmes: Another twist", *BIS Quarterly Review*, March, pp.23-30, *www.bis.org/publ/qtrpdf/r_qt1203e.pdf*.

OECD (2015), *OECD Business and Finance Outlook 2015*, OECD Publishing, Paris, *http://dx.doi.org/10.1787/9789264234291-en*.

OECD (2015b), *OECD Economic Outlook*, OECD Publishing, Paris, *http://dx.doi.org/10.1787/eco_outlook-v2015-2-en*.

OECD (2015c), *Pension Markets in Focus 2015*, November, *www.oecd.org/daf/fin/private-pensions/Pension-Markets-in-Focus-2015.pdf*.

Saiki, A. and J. Frost, "Does Unconventional Monetary Policy Affect Inequality? Evidence from Japan", *CEP Council on Economic Policies Working Paper* 2014/2, October 2014, *www.cepweb.org/wp-content/uploads/CEP_WP_Unconventional_Monetary_Policy_and_Inequality.pdf*.

Schich, S. and Y. Aydin (2014), "Measurement and analysis of implicit guarantees for bank debt: OECD survey results", *OECD Journal: Financial Market Trends*, Vol. 2014/1, *http://dx.doi.org/10.1787/fmt-2014-5jxzbv3r9rf4*.

ANNEX 1.A1

Methods and sources

Regional aggregates

- Total OECD area denotes the following 34 countries: Australia, Austria, Belgium, Canada, Chile, Czech Republic, Denmark, Estonia, Finland, France, Germany, Greece, Hungary, Iceland, Ireland, Israel Italy, Japan, Korea, Luxembourg, Mexico, Netherlands, New Zealand, Norway, Poland, Portugal, Slovak Republic, Slovenia, Spain, Sweden, Switzerland, Turkey, the United Kingdom and the United States.
- The G7 includes seven countries: Canada, France, Germany, Italy, Japan, United Kingdom and the United States.
- The OECD euro area includes 15 countries: Austria, Belgium, Estonia, Finland, France, Germany, Greece, Ireland, Italy, Luxembourg, Netherlands, Portugal, Slovak Republic, Slovenia and Spain.
- The Other OECD group includes fifteen countries: Australia, Chile, Czech Republic, Denmark, Hungary, Iceland, Israel, Korea, Mexico, New Zealand, Norway, Poland, Sweden, Switzerland and Turkey.

Calculations, definitions and data sources

- Gross borrowing requirements (GBR) as a percentage of GDP is calculated using nominal GDP data from the *OECD Economic Outlook* 98, November 2015.
- To facilitate comparisons with previous Outlooks, figures are converted into US dollars using exchange rates from 1 December 2009, unless indicated otherwise. Where figures are converted into US dollars using flexible exchange rates, the main text refers to that approach explicitly. Source: Thompson Reuters Datastream.
- All figures refer to calendar years.
- Aggregate figures for gross borrowing requirements (GBR), net borrowing requirements (NBR), central government marketable debt, redemptions, and debt maturing are compiled from the answers to the Borrowing Survey. The Secretariat inserted its own estimates/projections in cases of missing information for 2015 and/or 2016, using publicly available official information on redemptions and central government budget balances.

Chapter 2

Primary market developments for government bonds

This chapter discusses the functioning of primary markets, in particular by providing an overview of recent changes in issuing strategies, procedures and techniques, in response to regulatory changes and their impacts on issuance. Some of these changes, while understandable, might pose new challenges for debt managers. To the extent that debt managers are becoming more opportunistic, issuance programmes will be less predictable. That situation may not be desirable in the longer term. Debt management offices (DMOs) emphasize therefore that they aim at using a transparent debt management framework, supported by a strong communication policy. In this context, some DMOs took concrete steps to increase the predictability and transparency of their primary market operations.

The statistical data for Israel are supplied by and under the responsibility of the relevant Israeli authorities. The use of such data by the OECD is without prejudice to the status of the Golan Heights, East Jerusalem and Israeli settlements in the West Bank under the terms of international law.

2.1. Introduction

This chapter* focusses on the functioning of primary markets by discussing the main empirical results from the 2015 survey on primary market developments for government bonds. As of 31 July 2015, 32 OECD countries out of 34 replied to the survey.

Key findings:

- Debt management offices (DMOs) in OECD countries are using broadly similar issuance procedures and policies and are pursuing a high degree of transparency[1] and predictability that facilitate and encourage liquid markets. Broad and deep primary and secondary markets, in turn, are instrumental in lowering the cost of borrowing for the government.[2]
- The global financial and economic crisis had, and is having, an important impact on sovereign debt markets and borrowing activities and has led to changes in (the use of) issuance procedures and techniques. However, since issuance conditions vary among countries, the overall policy response and/or (changes in) the use of issuance techniques may differ. Most of DMOs have increased frequency of auctions, while some of them introduced post auction option facility and mini-tenders to the investors.
- DMOs consider issuing new instruments for various reasons including diversification of the investor base and enhancing liquidity of the government securities. Since January 2014, 18 OECD DMOs have started to issue new funding instruments such as inflation linked bonds, floating rate notes (FRN) and ultra-long bonds.
- Country overview of the potential implications of the new regulations such as Basel III, Volcker Rule and Solvency II on the functioning of the primary markets suggests that these new regulations could adversely affect market liquidity and demand for government securities. There are examples of banks, who have decided to downscale fixed income business including primary dealer activities in Belgium, Finland, Ireland and Denmark. However, it is difficult to quantify their full impact on primary markets of government bonds at this stage.

2.2. Overview of issuing procedures in the OECD area

The principal issuing procedure in use is auctions (Table 2.1). For example, the UK DMO is using auctions as the primary method of issuance for gilts across the maturity curve with conventional gilts and T-bills being issued via bid-price auctions. The responses show that 27 OECD countries (84%) are using auctions for issuing long-term, while 28 DMOs (88%) also are employing auctions for issuing short-term debt. 22 OECD countries (70%) show that the preferred auction type is the multiple-price format[3]. However, single-price[4] auctions run a close second. Moreover, 12 OECD countries use both single and multiple prices,

* Chapter written by Hans J. Blommestein with research and statistical support by Perla Ibarlucea Flores. Tables and figures are based on responses to the 2015 survey on "primary market developments for government bonds" by the OECD WPDM (cut-off date 31 October, 2015).

Table 2.1. **Overview of issuing procedures in the OECD area**

	Auctions		Auction type		Tap issues		Syndication
	Long-term	Short-term	Single-price	Multiple-price	Long-term	Short-term	
Australia	X	X		X			X
Austria	X			X	X	X	X
Belgium	X	X		X	X	X	X
Canada	X	X	X	X			X
Chile	X		X				
Czech Republic	X	X	X	X	X		X
Denmark	X	X	X		X		X
Finland	X		X		X	X	X
France	X	X		X	X	X	X
Germany	X	X		X	X	X	X
Greece[1]		X	X				
Hungary	X	X		X	X	X	X
Iceland	X	X	X				X
Ireland	X	X	X	Possible	X	X	X
Israel	X	X		X	X	X	
Italy	X	X	X	X	X	X	X
Japan	X	X	X	X			
Korea							
Luxembourg							X
Mexico	X	X	X	X	X	X	X
Netherlands	X	X	X	X	X	X	
New Zealand	X	X		X			X
Norway	X	X	X				
Poland	X	X	X	X			X
Portugal		X	X	X	X	X	X
Slovak Republic	X	X	Only T-Bills	X	X	X	X
Slovenia		X	X		X		X
Spain	X	X	Mixture	Mixture	X	X	X
Sweden	X	X		X		X	X
Switzerland	X	X	X				
Turkey[2]		X		X			
United Kingdom	X	X	X	X	X	X	X
United States	X	X	X				
Total	**27**	**28**	**21**	**22**	**18**	**16**	**23**

Table 2.1. **Overview of issuing procedures in the OECD area (continuation with country notes)**

Australia	Syndication is used on a selective basis. It is typically undertaken when there is a higher than normal level of risk associated with the issue of a new bond line (for example when issuing a bond line that extends the yield curve) or when there is a desire to issue a large volume of bonds in order to immediately establish a large liquid bond line.
Austria	In general, syndications are used for new issues. Existing issues are regularly tapped via scheduled auctions.
Belgium	Auctions are done through the "Bloomberg Auction System (BAS)" for two standard products, the short-term Treasury Certificates and long-term Linear Bonds. CP and "Schuldschein" programmes are done via tap issuance. The EMTN-programme allows syndications and tap issuance.
Canada	Syndication used for foreign currency debt issuance (for foreign exchange reserve funding purposes only) and for previous tactical issuances of a 50-year bond. A single price auction format is used only for issuance of inflation-linked bonds.
Chile	The Chilean Ministry of Finance considers bonds with maturity less than 365 days to be short term bonds. The procedure for local bonds is a Dutch auction.
Czech Republic	Syndication is used for long term foreign currency debt issuance. Single-price auction is used for T-bills, multiple-price auctions for bonds and tap sales, while fixed price is employed for buy-backs.

Table 2.1. **Overview of issuing procedures in the OECD area (continuation with country notes)**

Denmark	Primary dealer obligations do not require primary dealers to participate in auctions for a specified amount. Syndications are used for long term foreign currency debt issuance only, while short-term foreign paper is issued via Commercial Paper (CP) programmes.
France	Syndication is usually used once a year, essentially for the first issuance of a new line of long duration nominal bonds or long-term indexed bonds.
Germany	Syndication was used for the initial issuance of a linker and its first re-opening (2006) as well as for the first issuance of a 30-year linker (2015). Syndication is used for USD Bonds. Syndication was used for the Bund-Länder-Anleihe (2013).
Greece	Switch to single price auctions for T-bills. Switch to monthly auctions for T-bills instead of quarterly. Since May 2011, Greece is under EU/IMF support mechanism issuing only T-bills (13-week and 26-week Treasury bills).
Hungary	Some T-bills and bonds are sold via tap issuance or via subscriptions for retail investors. Syndication is used for the issuance of foreign exchange debt.
Iceland	Single price format used for T-bills and T-bonds. Syndication is used for the issuance of external debt.
Israel	Issuance of T-bills, nominal bonds and CPI-linked bonds. Issuer also uses switch auctions (redemption of short-term bonds and issuance of long-term bonds according to a conversion ratio) and buy-back auctions. Introduction of the use of primary dealers for CPI-linked bonds. More emphasis on investor relations, particularly on strategic investors from Asia. A 30-year fixed rate bond was issued for the first time in the beginning of 2012.
Italy	Syndication is used for the first tranches of long term bonds (both nominal and linkers) and for global USD bonds. Otherwise, single-price auctions are employed for selling and for tap issues. However, BOTs (Treasury bills) are issued with a multi-price auction mechanism. Bonds that are privately placed are issued through reverse enquiries.
Japan	Single-price auctions are used for 40-Year Bonds and 10-Year Inflation-Indexed Bonds (JGBi).
Korea	Information N.A.
Mexico	Syndication is used to launch new benchmarks of Fixed-rate and Inflation-linked bonds with a maturity longer than 3 years. Tap issues are executed through single-price auctions (Fixed-rate and Inflation-linked bonds), while multiple-price auctions are used for Cetes (T-Bills) and Floating-rate bonds (Bondes D).
Netherlands	For the new issuance of longer dated bonds, the DSTA uses the Dutch Direct Auction (DDA) system. The DDA system is implemented as a rule-based auction in which the DSTA is the book runner. End investors have the possibility to participate directly in auctions.
New Zealand	New Zealand continues to focus on extending the average maturity of the debt portfolio, in part by committing to the Inflation-indexed bond market through developing new maturities and regular tender issuance. Syndication continues to be a feature of new bond launches. In addition, 2014 New Zealand introduced a buy-back programme for the next maturing nominal bond (15 April 2015), which resulted in nearly NZD 4.0 billion being repurchased to help manage the maturity down from a record NZD 10.8 billion to NZD 7.2 billion.
Poland	Single-price auction are used for selling i) T-bills and T-bonds; ii) switches of T-bonds; and iii) supplementary auctions. Multiple price auctions are used for buy-backs. Syndication is used for the issuance of bonds in foreign markets.
Portugal	Portugal sells securities using multiple-price auctions for Treasury bills and single-price auctions for government bonds. Syndication is used for new issues at the longer end.
Slovak Republic	Syndication is used for i) the opening of new benchmark bond lines and ii) for issuing internationally (Switzerland, United States and Japan). Auctions are used for the tapping of all available lines of T-bonds and T-bills. Single-price auctions are used for T-bills.
Slovenia	Uniform price auctions are used for shorter-term securities (Treasury bills). 18-months Treasury bills have been issued since 2013. Tap issues of 12-month Treasury bills were introduced in 2012, but have not been used in the following years. The Bloomberg Auction System (BAS) is in place for long term government securities. However, no government bonds have been sold since the beginning of 2007. Thus far, only syndications have been used for issuing government bonds. However, auctions for issuing government bonds may be re-introduced as part of the next funding programme. Also tap issues of bonds can be used as a funding instrument, but, thus far, have only been for the recapitalisation of the Slovenian banking system in 2013 and 2014. However, in the future the government might decide to use taps (using auctions or syndications).
Spain	Spanish auctions follow a "Spanish-style" system (similar to a "modified-Dutch" system), involving a format that is a mixture of single-price and multiple-price auctions. Bids at a price above the weighted average price are awarded at the weighted average price, while bids at a price below the weighted average (but above the marginal price) are awarded at the bid price.
Sweden	Syndications are mainly used for issues in foreign currencies and, occasionally, for local currency government securities. A new 17-year linker was syndicated in April 2015 through a switch of a short-dated inflation-linked bond.
Switzerland	After auctions in 2012 (September) and 2013 (January) when the Swiss Federal Treasury reopened the Bond with maturity in 2015 (term to maturity 2.7 and 2.4 years) it was the longest maturity debt that has been sold directly to investors at negative yields. At the April 2015 auction, the Swiss Federal Treasury issued a 10-year bond at a negative yield of -0.055%.
Turkey[2]	Eurobond issuances are syndicated offerings arranged by book runners on a best-effort basis. The process includes the direct sale to banks and institutional investors on a book-building basis.

Table 2.1. **Overview of issuing procedures in the OECD area (continuation with country notes)**

United Kingdom	Auctions are the primary method of issuance for gilts across the maturity curve. Index-linked gilts are issued using a single price format while conventional gilts and T-bills are issued via bid-price auctions. Taps for market management are reserved for exceptional circumstances only. Taps are distinct from mini-tenders, which were introduced in October 2008 as one of the supplementary methods for distributing gilts. A programme of syndications was introduced in the 2009-10 financial year and has been used every year since then.
United States	U.S. Treasury reopens issues, but does so through regular and predictable auctions.

1. The Greek response is from the 2012 Survey of the OECD WPDM. At the cut-of date of this publication, Greece had no access to long-term funding markets. For more details *see www.pdma.gr/index.php/en/debt-instruments-greek-government-bonds*.
2. Turkish information refers to domestic debt operations only.
3. Estonia is not included in this survey because the Government of Estonia has not issued any securities since June 2002.

Source: Responses to the 2015 survey on primary markets developments by the OECD Working Party on Public Debt Management.

depending on the maturity or type of debt instruments. For example, some countries issue index-linked bonds using the single price format (e.g. Canada, Japan, Mexico and United Kingdom), while nominal bonds are issued via multiple price auctions. The U.S. Treasury reopens issues, but does so through regular and predictable auctions.

Table 2.1 also show that syndication is a commonly used issuance procedure (23 OECD countries are currently using syndications). For example, a programme of syndications was introduced by the UK DMO in the 2009-10 financial year and has been used every year since then.

The country notes of Table 2.1 indicate that syndication is mostly used for i) international bond issues (e.g. Canada, Czech Republic, Denmark, Hungary, Iceland, Italy, Poland, Slovak Republic, Sweden and Turkey); ii) the first-time issuance of new instruments (e.g. Australia, Austria, France, Germany, Mexico and New Zealand); iii) long(er)-dated bonds (e.g. Australia, Italy and France) and/or the sale of first tranches of benchmark issues, and iv) targeting and directly placing securities among specific investor groups.

More in general, syndications are often used on a highly selective basis. For example, it is typically undertaken by the Australian DMO when there is a higher than normal level of risk associated with the issue of a new bond line (for example when issuing a bond line that extends the yield curve) or when there is a desire to issue a large volume of bonds in order to immediately establish a large liquid bond line. In Canada, syndication are used for foreign currency debt issuance (for foreign exchange reserve funding purposes only) and for previous tactical issuances of a 50-year bond.

Syndications are likely to yield better results (higher placing certainty) in difficult market conditions. On the other hand, syndications are less transparent than auctions.

Tap issues are less frequently used, with 16 OECD DMOs (50%) using taps for issuing short-term debt and 18 DMOs (56%) for issuing long-term debt. In the UK, taps for market management are reserved for exceptional circumstances only. (Taps are distinct from mini-tenders, which were introduced by the UK DMO in October 2008 as one of the supplementary methods for distributing gilts.) In addition, a few countries use other techniques like private placement (e.g. Italy and Spain).

Lastly, issuance procedures and choice of instruments usually reflect the underlying debt management strategy. For example, the New Zealand DMO continues to focus on extending the average maturity of the debt portfolio, in part by committing to the inflation-indexed bond market through developing new maturities and regular tender issuance. Syndication continues to be a feature of new bond launches. In addition, 2014 New Zealand introduced a buy-back programme for the next maturing nominal bond (15 April 2015), which resulted in nearly NZD 4.0 billion being repurchased to help manage the maturity down from a record NZD 10.8 billion to NZD 7.2 billion. For the new issuance of longer dated bonds, the Dutch DMO uses the Dutch Direct Auction (DDA) system. The DDA system is implemented as a rule-based auction in which the DMO is the book runner.

2.3. Overview of recent changes in issuing procedures and techniques in OECD countries

As noted, issuance strategies and associated procedures are broadly similar (Table 2.1). However, they may vary greatly in terms of operational and technical details. Moreover, as a result of the great financial crisis and, later on, because of responses to the economic crisis, many countries have changed one or more (technical or operational) features of their issuance procedures. Table 2.2 provides a country-by-country overview of important changes made in issuance procedures and techniques.

Table 2.2. **Overview of recent changes in issuing procedures and techniques in OECD countries**

	Changes in issuing procedures and techniques
Australia	Auctions for all debt securities issued by the Australian Government are conducted on a multiple price basis.
Austria	In 2015, the legal possibility to issue Floating Rate Notes (using a domestic format [RAGB]) was introduced.
Belgium	The issuance strategy continues to be a combination of predictability and flexibility in order to respond adequately to a changing market environment, while managing uncertainty by maintaining sufficient predictability. The only change in Belgium's issuing procedures and techniques is the cancellation in 2014 of the two issuance techniques that were introduced in 2012 (syndicated taps for longer term "Linear bonds (OLO)" benchmarks, and Optional Reverse Inquiry Auctions [ORI auctions] for off-the-run OLOs at predetermined dates). Improved liquidity and lower funding needs made these two issuance techniques less useful.
Canada	In 2014-15, the Canadian government began issuing 50-year bonds through syndication.
Chile	Local market. From 2007 and onward, annual preannounced calendars containing fixed amounts (with the flexibility to diminish amounts by 20% or, alternatively, no allocation) and dates, using uniform price auctions. From 2003 and onward, nominal and inflation indexed bonds are on offer. In order to attract foreign investors, the number of auctions has been diminished, while increasing the amount for each auction. International market. The first global issuance of local currency securities and USD denominated bonds took place in 2010. In 2011 there was another issuance of USD denominated bonds as well as the re-opening of the globally issued local currency bond. The financial year of 2012 saw the issuance of USD denominated bonds with, respectively, 10 years and 30 years to maturity. It was the first time that Chile issued USD denominated bonds with 30 years to maturity. Since 2014, Chile issued two times in Euros with 10 years and 15 years to maturity.
Czech Republic	The situation is almost similar to those in last years: flexible auction calendars (monthly); double-bond auctions with volume range; regular meetings with primary dealers; indicative issuance volumes. The only change is the introduction of T+2 settlement time for auctions.
Denmark	No change in the procedure for issuing bonds (auctions supplemented with tap). Normally, two auctions are held each month in which two bond series are open for sale. As of January 2015, T-bills auctions are held twice per month: mid-month and end-of-month (previously only end-of-month).
Finland	Continued diversification of funding sources. Since the start of QE in the Eurosystem, the monitoring of market liquidity has become more important.
France	The following measures to increase flexibility and for better dealing with volatile market conditions were introduced at the end of 2007): 1) more "off the run" issuances, 2) higher issuance amounts at each auction, 3) more flexibility regarding issuance size with a wider range announced for the total amount to be issued, 4) two-optional auction dates (in August and December) and 5) changes in syndication vs. auction practices: less linkers (15-years) and more new issues of long-term (more than 30-years) bonds. The volume of to be auctioned securities is being announced as a (volume) range. The 7-year maturity bond can now be issued at both long-term and medium-term auctions. Finally, more efforts are spent on maintaining good investor relations.
Germany	Introduction of new 30-years segment for inflation linked federal securities

Table 2.2. Overview of recent changes in issuing procedures and techniques in OECD countries (cont.)

	Changes in issuing procedures and techniques
Hungary	Significant increase in the issuance of floating rate bonds. Coupons of the newly issued floating rate bonds are linked to the 3-month BUBOR money market rate, instead of the previous practice, where the yield of 3-month T-Bill auctions was the basis of the coupon. The 50% purchase limit for Primary dealers on T-Bill auctions has been abolished, however in case of bond auctions this rule still exists.
Iceland	During the last few years, there is a greater emphasis on maintaining good investor relations, including via regular meetings with institutional and foreign investors. The co-ordination with PDs has been improved. A more flexible auction calendar has been introduced. Normally, there are now two bond auctions per month instead of one, while the number of series offered in each auction has been increased from one up to three. Longer dated bonds have been introduced. Since 2011, a medium term debt strategy has been published annually.
Ireland	Return to full market access following exit from EU/IMF programme at end 2013. Regular schedule of single price auctions.
Israel	Issuance of off-the-run bonds via switch auctions. Introducing PDs for CPI linked bonds. More emphasis on maintaining good investor relations. Introduction of extended T-bill programme.
Italy	There are no changes in issuing procedures. Since the end of 2011, auctions of CTZ (the two-year zero coupon bond) are priced using a discretionary pricing model. This model has already been adopted for all single-price auctions, whereby the issuer sets discretionary the total auction amount (which corresponds to a marginal clearing price) within a range previously communicated to the market when the auction was announced. In addition, from the second quarter of 2012 there has been a 5% increase in non-competitive re-openings reserved for the Government Bond Specialists (the Primary Dealers). Access to this additional 5% is linked to the performance by the primary dealers on the secondary market. The previous dual (separate) communication strategy for auctioning medium-term and long-term bonds (the first message entails an announcement about the bonds on offer to the market and the second one an announcement about the auction amounts) was replaced by a single announcement incorporating both messages (both bonds on offer and the amounts to be auctioned). Moreover, T-bills, which are auctioned on a yield basis, are no longer offered together with the CTZ; T-bills are auctioned on a price basis (they are offered together with BTP[euro] i). Starting in 2013, floating rate notes (CCTeu) are issued on a monthly basis, instead of quarterly as in 2012. Since March 2012 the Italian Treasury has been issuing a new retail bond via a regulated retail platform; this bond is a government security indexed to the Italian inflation rate (BTP Italia), with semi-annual coupons and a maturity of four years.
Japan	The following changes in issuing rules have been adopted in April 2015: 1) In order to maintain and enhance the liquidity of the JGB secondary market, the amount of Auctions for Enhanced-Liquidity was increased from 700 billion yen per month to 800 billion yen per month. 2) In order to ensure the stable issuance of JGBs, the maximum amount of bidding by each auction participant was decreased to one-half of the planned issuance amount, while the obligation of JGB Market Special Participants (primary dealers) to bid has been raised to 4% or more of the planned issuance amount. 3) The 10-year Bond line will normally be reopened except in cases where interest rates are fluctuating significantly.
Luxembourg	Luxembourg has only issued syndicated bonds during the last couple of years. There are no plans to change this policy.
Mexico	The use of syndications as a funding tool in the local market began in 2010. In July 2011, this tool was changed from syndication based on "book building", to a syndication based on an "auction mechanism".
Netherlands	Introduction of an USD Commercial Paper programme (USCP).
New Zealand	The introduction of reverse tenders in April 2015. The New Zealand DMO recently made changes to the quarterly bond tender schedule by including the specific maturity likely to be offered at tender, providing additional predictability to their issuance activity.
Norway	In 2014, Norway began to issue each year a new 10-year bond. Previously, an 11-year bond was introduced every second year.
Poland	Changes in rules for switching auctions were implemented on the 1st October, 2013.These modifications to switches included: 1) introduction of a single- price formula for T-bond switching auctions; 2) introduction of the possibility of placing non-competitive bids; and 3) introduction of the possibility of cash purchases of T-bonds after switching auctions.
Portugal	Portugal returned in 2014 to the long end of the market by issuing long-term instruments using auctions (after exiting the Economic and Financial Assistance Programme). This return to the market included the introduction of a single-price technique. Recently, Portugal used for the first time a dual-tranche syndicated issue.
Slovak Republic	Introduction of T+2 settlement time for auctions of both T-bills and T-bonds. This change is in line with the harmonisation process in the Eurozone.
Slovenia	The execution methods and procedures for buybacks and exchange transactions were revised as part of the 2015 funding programme. A *Delivery Versus Payment* (DVP) settlement of T-bills auctions was introduced in October 2014. It is envisaged to introduce this DVP mechanism also for auctions of T-bonds. There was more emphasis on investor relations (IR) via i) recurrent investor meetings, ii) more frequent participations in conferences and other investor-focused events, iii) regular updates of an IR specific website, and iv) the regular distribution of a newsletter and the electronic distribution targeted information to investors. Auctions of government bonds (primarily for taps of existing bonds) might be re-introduced in the near future. Opportunities for the execution of exchanges, switches, buybacks and other liability management operations are being monitored on an on-going basis.

Table 2.2. **Overview of recent changes in issuing procedures and techniques in OECD countries** *(cont.)*

	Changes in issuing procedures and techniques
Spain	Syndications are used for 1) new issues of 10-year, 15-year and 30-year nominal Euro benchmarks; 2) new issues of European HICP-linked bonds; 3) for foreign currency EMTN (Euro Medium Term Notes) benchmarks; and for 4) "niche" products (e.g. FRNs). Regular auctions (part of the auction calendar) are used for i) T-bills (new issues and taps); ii) new issues of 3-year and 5-year nominal benchmarks; iii) and taps of all Euro benchmarks. Special auctions have been used for small taps of specific bonds; they are not part of the regular auction calendar, without Primary Dealer obligations. These special operations are designed to create liquidity at certain parts of the yield curve. Private placements are normally used for small allocations of so-called "niche" products.
Sweden	In the first half of 2015, the Swedish National Debt Office has split the issue volume of their regular auctions into two different maturities in order to meet the demand in different segments. The volumes are unchanged in order to ensure stability in the Swedish Government Bond market. The issuance of inflation-linked bonds is unchanged. However, the Debt Office's long-term ambition is to increase the number of maturities, thereby avoiding excessive concentrations at specific points of the yield curve. The objective is that no single linker exceeds 30 per cent of the domestic inflation-linked bond index.
Switzerland	Recently, the window (subscription time) for auctioning T-Bonds was standardised (by shortening it by 1 hour), making it identical to the window for T-Bills. Auction participants have now the same window to submit bids (from 9.30 am till 11.00 am). The response to this change has been very favourable. Since August 2011 bids with prices above 100 per cent have been allowed. The financial market crisis and the resulting flight to safety saw tender prices regularly rising above par, enabling the Swiss government to raise money with negative yields.
Turkey	In addition to conventional USD and EUR denominated bond issuances, Turkey has been issuing Sukuk bonds both in domestic and international markets since 2012 as part of the effort to broaden the investor base. Apart from Sukuk bonds, Turkey re-introduced in 2011 bond issues in the Japanese Yen Samurai Bond market under the JBIC (Japanese Bank for International Cooperation) GATE guarantee facility. Under this JBIC guarantee scheme, the Turkish Treasury has issued three Samurai bonds (since 2011). Turkey also did a private placement in the Samurai Market in 2013. The 2015 domestic borrowing strategy is focused on Turkish Lira (TL) denominated 2, 5 and 10-year fixed rate coupon bonds issued as "benchmark bonds". In addition, Turkey has been issuing every month TL denominated 5-year fixed rate coupon benchmark bonds (except in December in 2015).
United Kingdom	Auctions remain the primary method of issuance for gilts across the maturity curve. A post auction option facility, that allows successful bidders to purchase additional stock of up to 10% of the amount allocated at auction, was introduced with effect from June 2009 and has continued to be offered since then. The current planning assumption is that auctions will deliver 78% of total gilt sales in 2015-16. The syndication programme will continue to be used in 2015-16 to launch new gilts and/or for re-openings of high duration gilts. The DMO envisages holding approximately six syndicated offerings (four index-linked and two long conventional) in the financial year (with at least one transaction per quarter). Syndications enable the DMO to retain flexibility in aligning demand with supply as each syndication is sized taking into account the size and quality of end-investor demand. Mini-tenders, which were introduced with effect from October 2008 as a more flexible supplementary distribution method, may be scheduled in 2015-16 depending on market demand communicated to the DMO and the progress of the progress of the supplementary issuance programme.

Source: Responses to the 2015 survey on primary markets developments by the OECD Working Party on Public Debt Management.

Many DMOs have initially adopted changes in issuance procedures so as to address (some of) the issuance challenges associated with the strong increase in borrowing needs in the wake of the great crisis. Other sources of issuance challenges emerged later on and include QE programmes and concerns about the adverse impact of new regulations on market-making by primary dealers and market liquidity. Some countries have adopted issuing rules and special auctions outside the regular auction calendar so as to enhance liquidity in their government bond markets.

More specifically, delegates from the OECD Working Party on Public Debt Management confirmed the following trends and developments:

i. Changes in issuance methods and procedures, including more flexible auction calendars (weekly or monthly instead of quarterly/annual) and using other distribution methods than "regular" auctions including mini-tenders, syndication, Dutch Direct Auction (DDA) procedures and private placement. (See Table 2.2 for a country-by-country overview.)

ii. In response to uncertainty and market volatility, auction calendars have become more flexible in most jurisdictions; auctions were held more frequently (e.g. Denmark and Iceland); and more bond lines, issued at each auction, were introduced (e.g. France and Iceland). The UKDMO noted that auctions remain the primary method of issuance for gilts across the maturity curve. But the DMO also introduced new issuing procedures such as a post auction option facility; this facility allows successful bidders to purchase additional stock of up to 10% of the amount allocated at auction; it was introduced with effect from June 2009 and has continued to be offered since then. Moreover, with effect from October 2008 the UKDMO introduced mini-tenders as a more flexible supplementary distribution method.

iii. In order to smooth the redemption profile, some countries introduced new maturities. For example:

- Germany introduced a new structure of maturities for 30-years segment for inflation linked federal securities.
- Canada began issuing a 50-year bond.
- France introduced more new issues of long-term bonds (more than 30 years).

iv. Some countries also issue more frequently off-the-run bonds in order to provide liquidity and create smooth redemption flows. For example, Belgium, France and Japan have increased the number of re-openings (of off-the-run bonds that have sufficient market demand) so as to reduce market volatility, and (in the case of Japan) to enhance liquidity of the JGB market.

v. Ireland saw the return to full market access following exit from EU/IMF programme at the end of 2013, with the Irish DMO using a regular schedule of single price auctions.

vi. Other changes in issuance strategies include: i) a stronger emphasis on retail issuance (e.g. in Italy where a new bond is issued through a regulated retail platform) so as to broaden and to increase the stability of the investor base; ii) in order to attract foreign investors, several DMOs have reduced the number of auctions while the amount per auction has been increased (e.g. Chile); and iii) more emphasis on investor relations via:

- more frequent meetings with investors,
- more frequent participations in investor-focused events such as conferences on public borrowing operations and government debt issues,
- more frequent updates of specific websites focused on investor relations,
- and via regular publication of newsletters, distributed via regular mail or via individual electronic distribution to investors (e.g. Czech Republic, Israel, Slovenia, France and Iceland).

Some of these changes, while understandable, might create risks. To the extent that debt managers are becoming more opportunistic, issuance programmes will be less predictable. That situation may not be desirable in the longer term. DMOs emphasise therefore that they aim at using a transparent debt management framework, supported by a strong communication policy. In this context, some DMOs took concrete steps to increase the predictability and transparency of their primary market operations. For example, the New Zealand DMO recently made changes to the quarterly bond tender schedule by including the specific maturity likely to be offered at tender, thereby providing additional predictability to their issuance activity.

Transparency and predictability are instrumental in reducing the type of market noise that may unnecessarily increase borrowing costs. In this context, DMOs are using issuance strategies that reflect a balance between predictability and flexibility. The latter feature contributes to an opportunistic response to a changing market environment, while predictability is meant to reduce uncertainty for dealers and investors. From this perspective changes in issuing procedures and techniques mirror changes in the balance between predictability and flexibility.

For example, the syndication programme of the UKDMO will continue to be used in 2015-16 to launch new gilts and/or for re-openings of high duration gilts. Syndications enable the DMO to retain flexibility in aligning demand with supply as each syndication is sized taking into account the size and quality of end-investor demand.

2.4. Issuance of new instruments

In this part of the survey, DMOs were asked whether they have issued new types of securities such as inflation-linked bonds, variable rate notes, longer dated securities, etc. since January 2014. However, some countries reported also funding instruments that were introduced at a somewhat earlier stage. For example, Japan reported that new types of securities were issued between September 2013 and December 2013.

New instruments are issued for various reasons, but mostly for the widening and diversification of the investor base. Enhancing liquidity at various points of the yield curve was also mentioned in some cases. The strong increase in borrowing needs played an important role in aiming for a broader investor base in quite a few jurisdictions.

In the period September 2013-July 2015, 58% of OECD issuers (18 countries) have introduced new instruments (see Table 2.3).

Table 2.3. **Issuance of new government securities by DMOs (since January 2014)**

YES	NO
58%	42%
Austria	Australia
Belgium	Czech Republic
Canada	Denmark
Chile	Finland
Germany	France
Hungary	Iceland
Ireland	Israel
Italy	Mexico
Japan	Netherlands
Luxembourg	Norway
New Zealand	Poland
Portugal	Sweden
Slovak Republic	Switzerland
Slovenia	
Spain	
Turkey	
United Kingdom	
United States	

Source: Responses to the 2015 survey on primary markets developments by the OECD Working Party on Public Debt Management.

2.5. Which new types of funding instruments were issued (since January 2014)?

Table 2.4 refers to the issuance of new funding instruments by 18 OECD DMOs such as (long-term) linker issuance, floating rate notes (FRNs), and ultra-long instruments. In addition, some OECD countries began to issue "Sukuk" bonds (i.e. Luxembourg, Turkey and

Table 2.4. **Which new types of funding instruments were issued by DMOs (since January 2014)?**

Inflation linked bonds	Variable rate notes	Longer dated securities	Others
Belgium	Austria	Canada	Luxembourg
Germany	Hungary	Ireland	Portugal
Japan	United States	New Zealand	Slovak Republic
Spain		Portugal	Turkey
		Slovenia	United Kingdom
		Spain	

Table 2.4. **Which new types of funding instruments were issued by DMOs (since January 2014)? (continuation with country notes)**

Austria	EUR FRN (Floating Rate Note) in EMTN (Euro Medium Term Notes) format issued in 2014.
Belgium	Inflation linked bonds in an EMTN (Euro Medium Term Notes) format.
Chile	Issuance in Euros (10-year and 15-year).
Canada	50-year nominal bonds.
Germany	30-year linked bonds.
Hungary	New 3-year and 5-year floating rate HUF (Hungary Forint) bonds. Coupons are linked to 3-month BUBOR (Budapest Interbank Offered Rate). New 4-, 6- and 15-year floating rate bonds for retail investors. Coupons are linked to the 12-month T-bill auction yields.
Ireland	15-year and 30-year benchmark bonds.
Italy	Inflation linked bonds: 6-year and 8-year BTP Italia (in addition to the already existing 4-year maturity, BTP[euro] i and inflation linked EMTNs). Variable rate notes: The initial maturity of new CCTeu (Treasury Certificates indexed to Euribor) gradually moved towards the 7-year tenor. Longer dated securities: A 50-year EMTN in May 2013 and a 40-year EMTN in September 2013. Other instruments: A new 7-year BTP benchmark was introduced in October 2013.
Japan	New type of JGBi (Japanese Government Bond – Inflation-linked) has been issued since October 2013. For more details, see the press release: *www.mof.go.jp/english/jgbs/topics/press_release/20130621-04e.htm)*
Luxembourg	In October 2014, the Luxembourg Government issued a 200 000 000 five-year EUR denominated Sukuk bond with an Al-Ijara structure.
New Zealand	New April 2027-long-dated nominal bond (extending curve 4 years, launched by syndication) and new September 2035 IIB (extending the curve by 5 years, launched by a syndication).
Portugal	New 30-year (Jan15) and new EMTN – USD 10-year.
Slovak Republic	Issuance of NOK (Norwegian Krone) bonds and EUR private placement.
Slovenia	20-year bond issued in the 1st quarter of 2015.
Spain	The longer dated securities refer to a 50-year private placement.
Turkey	In November 2014, Turkey issued an international Sukuk with a maturity of 10-years (previous two issues had maturities of around 5 years).
United Kingdom	In June 2014, Britain became the first country outside the Islamic world to issue sovereign Sukuk when it sold GBP 200 million of Sukuk, maturing on 22 July 2019 to a wide range of investors including sovereign wealth funds, central banks and domestic and international financial institutions. Issuance of sovereign Sukuk is not part of the government's normal debt management policy but is designed to deliver wider benefits, including reinforcing London's status as the leading centre for Islamic finance outside of the Muslim world and promoting greater trade and investment into the United Kingdom. An ongoing programme is not envisaged at this stage. In October 2014, the UK government successfully issued a sovereign bond in China's currency, the renminbi (RMB), becoming the first western country to do so and issuing the largest ever non-Chinese RMB bond. The RMB 3 billion (approximately GBP 300 million) bond, has a maturity of 3 years and will be used to finance Britain's reserves of foreign currency. Currently, Britain only holds reserves in US dollars, euros, yen and Canadian dollars, so the issuance signals the RMB's potential as a future reserve currency. Britain's sovereign RMB bond is a stand-alone issuance; the government continues to meet its domestic financing requirements entirely in sterling.
United States	The U.S. Treasury began issuing a 2-year FRN in January 2014.

Source: Responses to the 2015 survey on primary markets developments by the OECD Working Party on Public Debt Management.

United Kingdom) which were sold to a wide range of investors including sovereign wealth funds, central banks and domestic and international financial institutions.

For some governments, the issuance of Sukuk bonds is not part of the government's regular or normal debt management policy. For example, the United Kingdom has started to issue sovereign "Sukuks" but this issuance programme is not associated with the UK's debt financing objectives. Instead, it is designed to deliver wider benefits like promoting greater trade and investment, largely driven by the Government's desire to cement the position of London and the UK as a centre of international – and Islamic – finance (see also Table 2.4).

The U.S. Treasury auctioned its first floating-rate note (FRN) in January 2014. With this sale, the government auctioned the first new marketable debt instrument since linkers (inflation-protected securities) were introduced in 1997. The new two-year FRN is a fixed-principal security with quarterly interest payments and interest rates indexed to the thirteen-week Treasury bill.

By adding this new product, the investor base will expand, which is likely to lower the government's borrowing cost.[5]

2.6. Plans of DMOs to sell in the future new types of securities

DMOs were also asked whether they are planning to issue new types of securities like inflation linked bonds, variable rate notes, longer dated securities, etc.

Thirty-one (31) responses were given. A majority of twenty-five (25) countries (or around 80%) answered that they were currently not planning to issue new types of securities (see Table 2.5). In essence, most plans to sell in the future new types of instruments mirror changes in debt management strategies. However, this is not always the case. As noted, the issuance of Sukuks by the UK DMO is not part of the government's normal debt management policy. Hence, the DMO is not envisaging an ongoing programme at this stage.

Table 2.5. **Plans of DMOs to sell in the future new types of securities**

YES	NO
19%	81%
Austria	Australia
Ireland	Belgium[1]
Luxembourg	Canada
New Zealand	Chile
Slovenia	Czech Republic
Turkey	Denmark
	Finland
	France
	Germany
	Hungary
	Iceland
	Israel
	Italy[2]
	Japan
	Mexico
	Netherlands
	Norway
	Poland
	Portugal
	Slovak Republic

Table 2.5. **Plans of DMOs to sell in the future new types of securities** *(cont.)*

YES	NO
19%	81%
	Spain
	Sweden
	Switzerland
	United Kingdom
	United States
6	25
Total answers	**31**

1. The Belgian Treasury is currently reviewing longer maturities as part of its funding strategy, but no decisions have been taken.
2. The Italian Treasury is currently not planning to issue new instruments, but keeps studying new types of government securities.

Source: Responses to the 2015 survey on primary markets developments by the OECD Working Party on Public Debt Management.

Hence, six DMOs (or nearly 20% of the respondents) indicated that they were planning to issue new types of funding instruments (Table 2.5), including variable rate notes and longer dated securities (see Table 2.6). For example, Austria is planning to issue floating rates notes under domestic law, New Zealand is planning to issue a 2033 nominal bond, while Slovenia will issue a 30-year government bond and is planning to use other instruments like the "Schuldschein[6]".

Table 2.6. **Details on the planned issuance of new types of instruments**

Variable rate notes	Longer dated securities	Others
Austria	Slovenia	Slovenia
	New Zealand	Ireland
	Turkey	Turkey

Notes:

Austria: Floating Rates Note (FRN) under domestic law (RAGB, Republic of Austria Government Bonds) may be issued.
Ireland: DMO continues to explore options such as longer dates securities, USD issuance and inflation linked bonds.
New Zealand: Longer-dated April 2033 nominal bond so as to extend the curve by 6 years.
Slovenia: A 30-year government bond, private placements of bonds and other established long-term financial market instruments such as "Schuldschein" and "Namensschuldverschreibung".
Turkey: Depending on market conditions (including demand by institutional investors), the government may consider issuing longer term Turkish Lira denominated bonds. Turkey is planning to issue a Yen denominated bond in Samurai market in 2015 (on a stand-alone basis).

Source: Responses to the 2015 survey on primary markets developments by the OECD Working Party on Public Debt Management.

In sum, higher borrowing needs have led to a greater diversification in the use of funding instruments, in particular via an increase in the issuance of inflation-linked bond issuances. This in turn has broadened the investor base. Continued funding challenges have led to a situation where a broad and diverse investor base is more essential than before. This means that it is more important to take into account the preferences of both foreign and domestic investors when making changes in issuance procedures and introducing new instruments. In this regard, most countries mention that they give a higher priority to maintaining good investor relationships.

2.7. The largest (expected) impact of new regulations on the functioning of primary markets

Table 2.7 is based on responses by DMOs to the question which new regulations have in their judgement the largest (expected or potential) impact on their primary markets. The table shows that many countries have quite different views on the severity of the impact of these regulations on their markets. Some countries (such as Chile, Hungary and Norway) expect a moderate influence of these new regulations. However, several other issuers note that, given the evolving nature of some of the regulatory changes, it is difficult to fully appreciate the effect that the new regulations will have on primary market operations. Moreover, many of the rules have not yet been implemented, thereby increasing the difficulty in ranking the impact of these new regulations.

Table 2.7. **Summary country overview of the largest (expected) impact of regulations on the functioning of primary government securities markets**

Tax on financial transactions (e.g. Tobin-tax)	Basel III	Volcker Rule	Shorting restrictions	Other regulations	Solvency II	New rules for swaps
Austria	Australia	Poland	Poland	Belgium	Switzerland	Netherlands
Czech Republic	Belgium		Turkey	Czech Republic		Norway
Denmark	France			Denmark		Turkey
Germany	Italy			Germany		
Hungary	Japan			Iceland		
Ireland	Poland			Mexico		
Ireland	Portugal			Netherlands		
Israel	Slovenia			Portugal		
Luxembourg	Spain			Slovenia		
Poland	Turkey			United Kingdom		
Portugal	United Kingdom					
Slovak Republic	United States					
Slovenia						
Sweden						
Turkey						

Source: Responses to the 2015 survey on primary markets developments by the OECD Working Party on Public Debt Management.

The category, "Other Regulations" that has a significant (expected) impact on the functioning of primary markets refers to a quite diverse set of regulations. In Belgium it covers regulations concerning the risk weighting of sovereign debt. In Denmark it denotes the Leverage Ratio framework. In Germany, UK and Slovenia it designates MiFID II/MiFIR (Markets in Financial Instruments Directive II and Regulation, MiFIR). In Iceland it refers to capital control rules. In the Netherlands it denotes BSRD (Bangko Sentral Registration Document), CSDR (Central Securities Depositories Regulation) and EMIR (European Markets Infrastructure Regulation). In Portugal this category covers the ESRB (European Systemic Risk Board) report on the regulatory treatment of sovereign exposures, the MiFID II and CSDR. In the Czech Republic it refers to the regulatory treatment of sovereign debt exposures. In Mexico the category "Other Regulations" refers to "The European Commission Proposal" (ECP), which prohibits proprietary trading operations by European banks, including their overseas subsidiaries. The prohibition excludes operations involving sovereign securities of the European Union. Moreover, trading operations (including market making) may need to be separated from the bank when certain thresholds are exceeded. The Mexican DMO also notes that the ECP seems to suggest that overseas subsidiaries may be exempt from the separation requirement when the banking group operates under a decentralized business strategy and authorities have agreed to apply a multiple point of entry (MPE) resolution strategy. (For more details about this regulation see European Commission "Proposal for a Regulation of the European Parliament and of the Council on structural measures improving the resilience of EU credit institutions", Brussels, 29.1.2014.)

Sovereign issuers have expressed on various occasions their concern about the impact (positive or negative) of new (or envisaged) financial reform measures. Most of the DMOs have expressed concerns that these new regulations could adversely affect 1) market liquidity and 2) the demand for government securities by end-investors (i.e., reduced demand by these investors). Table 2.8 provides a detailed, country-by-country overview of the largest (expected) impact of new regulations on the functioning of primary markets, including Basel III, Financial Transactions Tax (FTT), the Volcker rule, Solvency II, Shorting Restrictions, New Rules for Swaps and the category with quite diverse "Other Regulations".

New rules such as Basel III, Solvency II, short sale restrictions, and the Volcker rule, among others, are meant to reduce the occurrence of major financial instability episodes. On the other hand, several DMOs are arguing that they may reduce the capability of the banking system to warehouse and distribute government bonds, in particular during the first stages of their implementation and when not adequately fine-tuned. In general, the impact of these new regulations will be mostly felt in terms of higher transaction costs in the secondary market for government bonds. However, these increased costs will inevitably spill-over into the primary markets, both in terms of higher borrowing costs and lower quality in the execution of the placement of bonds.

The 2015 survey responses show that DMOs are mostly concerned about the tax on financial transactions (50%), followed by Basel III (42.9%). Figure 2.1 reflects the worries of sovereign issuers that these two categories of new regulations have potentially the biggest adverse impact on the functioning of primary markets.

Interestingly, Figure 2.1 also shows that only 3.6% of the DMOs considered the Volcker rule as having the biggest (potential) impact. Not surprisingly, the category capturing a rather diverse set of new regulations (denoted here as "Other Regulations") reflects the concerns of quite a few DMOs. (Figure 2.1 demonstrates that 35.7% of the respondents associate "Other regulations" with having potentially the biggest impact.)

The Survey and debate by the OECD Working Party on Public Debt Management about the impact of (envisaged) regulatory changes indicate that these new regulations will most likely contribute to shifts in the business models of banks, although the full impact of new regulations is not easy to quantify. For that reason, also the ranking of the impact of these new regulations may also be problematic. But some of the new regulations are likely to reduce the profitability (hence the attractiveness) of being a primary dealer in government securities markets and/or reduce the ability of primary dealers to actively participate in primary issuance and/or maintain sufficient inventories in government bonds (and thus provide liquidity in the different public bond markets). Indeed, there are examples of banks, who have decided to downscale fixed income business including primary dealer activities (see, for example, the situation in Belgium, Finland, Ireland and Denmark as reported in Table 2.8).

In terms of liquidity, Basel III outlines that countries should adopt two rules – the Liquidity Coverage Ratio (LCR) and the Net Stable Funding Ratio (NSFR). Together, it is not

Table 2.8. Country-by-country overview of regulations with the largest (expected) impact on primary markets

	Country-by country overview
Australia	This is difficult to evaluate at this time, although the impact of these regulations has been minor to date.
Austria	A possible change of the regulatory treatment of Sovereign Exposure could impact the liquidity and pricing of sovereign bonds.
Belgium	Regulatory reform adopted in the EU has delivered better capitalised, more resilient financial institutions and more stable financial markets. Key achievements include the main elements of CRD IV/CRR, which have addressed both the quality and quantity of regulatory capital, and thus improved the resilience of banks across the EU. Some of the key elements of MiFID II/MiFIR will improve transparency and disclosure requirements, which could improve competition and could provide better prices for market participants. However, regulatory initiatives, either individually or cumulatively, have the potential to result in a number of unintended (direct and indirect) consequences for sovereign debt markets, which should be carefully considered, assessed, and as appropriate, addressed. The cumulative impact of regulations on sovereign debt markets will likely lead to three possibly interlinked phenomena, some of which have already impacted sovereign debt markets. Firstly, changes in the capital requirements for primary dealers have led to a decline in the profitability and, therefore, potentially the sustainability of the market making model. This in turn has contributed to a reduction in liquidity in secondary markets, as fewer participants are willing to warehouse these assets in order to quote prices to buyers. Finally, changes brought about by the CRR and MIFID might have a detrimental long term impact on repo markets, and, therefore, the liquidity or even good-functioning of secondary sovereign debt markets. This reduction in liquidity leading to higher funding cost will be further intensified if the projected changes in the risk weighting of sovereign debt exposures in bank and insurance balance sheets will only consider the macro prudential aspect of sovereign debt exposures and omit to consider the important role of government bonds related to the financing a country and supporting its economy, hence its long term financial sustainability. The FTT has made its reappearance but in a light version not including sovereign debt or derivatives markets. However one should remain vigilant as political decision makers still aim at broadening the scope of this tax. Liquidity and warehousing capabilities of banks influence the pricing of bonds in secondary markets and ultimately the cost of funding.
Canada	Given the evolving nature of some of the regulatory changes, it is difficult to fully appreciate the impact that the new regulations will have on primary markets/operations in the debt management space. Many of the rules have not yet been fully implemented and, as such, are not observable. This means that the ranking of the impact of these new regulations is not feasible at this time. The information provided below gives a picture of potential effects of new regulations on our primary markets. *Volcker Rule.* The Volcker Rule prevents U.S. banks from engaging in proprietary trading on its own behalf (not on behalf of customers) in certain financial assets. The purpose of this rule is to reduce high-risk trading bets by large banks. Although this rule is yet to officially go into effect, there is potential for this rule to affect the Government of Canada primary issuance market. Since some banks will not be able to purchase Canadian Government securities there is concern that this could decrease the level of liquidity of these issues, thus increasing the cost of borrowing. *Solvency II.* While Solvency II requires insurance companies to manage all risks that affect their organization, it is not clear if this has had any impact on our primary market. It is possible there is more impact on the secondary market. *Basel III.* There are three areas that Basel III covers, which include capital, liquidity, and systematic risk. For Canada, the Office of the Superintendent of Financial Institutions (OFSI) sets the specific rules based on the Basel guidelines. In 2013, under the Capital Adequacy Requirements (CAR) Guidelines, OFSI required Canadian banks to meet target capital levels that equal or exceed the Basel III minimum capital requirements. In terms of liquidity, Basel III outlines that countries should adopt two rules - the Liquidity Coverage Ratio (LCR) and the Net Stable Funding Ratio (NSFR). Together, it is unclear what the full impact of Basel III on our primary market issuance will be. Our auction performance, which we generally evaluate using coverage ratio and the tail value (the cut-off yield minus the average yield), has been slightly affected by the departure of a few government securities distributors (GSDs). However, it is not clear that the GSDs left due to regulations or some other factor. Although there is no clear impact yet on our auction yields or coverage ratios, certain effects that are evident in our dealer markets, are the ability of dealers to act as market makers. Under Basel III, the capital requirements and liquidity requirements are causing dealers to hold more capital, which prevents them from cost effectively holding large amounts of securities and to act as principals in trades. As a result, investors are having a more difficult time to complete either side of a large trade. The implementation of Basel III has varied across jurisdictions, which may have had jurisdictional effects on how auction participants from different jurisdictions participate at our auction. *Shorting restrictions*, *Taxes on financial transactions*, and *New rules for swaps*: not applicable.
Chile	The Ministry of Finance is working on the implementation of Basel III. The Central Bank has begun with the liquidity regulation part, which is likely to increase the demand for Treasury securities (although its impact is likely to be moderate).
Czech Republic	Regulations are likely to result in lower demand for government bonds.
Denmark	Denmark noticed a drop in market liquidity but it is difficult to judge how much can be attributed to new regulations. There are examples of banks who have decided to downscale fixed income activities including primary dealer activities. Banks are adjusting their business models and are excluding low-margin business areas especially in smaller, less liquid government bond markets. The combined effect of new regulations and structural changes in the banking industry will most likely be less intense competition and less liquidity provision by primary dealers. Consequently, the market as a whole is expected to have a lower risk-absorbing capacity, which ultimately may lead to increased volatility and higher financing costs for DMOs. The decision to increase the frequency of Danish T-bill auctions in 2015 can be seen as an example of a policy change aimed at supporting market liquidity. In addition, the Danish DMO is more focused on using buy-backs, switches and taps to support market liquidity.
Finland	Without undertaking specific, in-depth studies, ranking the quantitative impact of new regulations remains a formidable challenge. It is clear, however, that some regulations are likely to have an adverse impact. Some of the new rules are likely to have an adverse influence on the market making environment for Finnish government securities, with a negative impact on market liquidity (for this reason work on this topic has been undertaken with the ESDM).

Table 2.8. Country-by-country overview of regulations with the largest (expected) impact on primary markets *(cont.)*

	Country-by country overview
France	*Volcker rule:* Exemptions in the final version of the US bill probably will mean that the participation of US banks in the French market for government securities should not too strongly affected. However, the actual impact of the Volcker rule remains to be assessed. *Solvency II:* its impact is expected to adversely affect the demand for instruments at the very long end of the yield curve (beyond 20 years). On the other hand, there might be an increase in the structural demand for long-term government bonds due to the need to fill duration gaps by insurance companies. *Basel III (CRD IV):* This regulation is expected to put more limits on the balance sheets of primary dealers to warehouse bonds. This in turn would imply higher market volatility, especially around auctions. On the other hand, the need for banks of holding HQLA would mean a higher structural demand for French bonds. *Shorting restrictions:* no impact. *New rules for swaps*: It is possible that there will be an increase in the demand for bonds for managing duration risk instead of using swaps.
Germany	Some of the new regulations (notably, *FTT, MiFID II and Basel III*) may reduce the demand for German Federal securities. The liquidity in the cash market for German Federal securities (as well as in the repo and the futures markets) might decrease. As a result, activities in the primary market may become more challenging: a) *The Financial Transactions Tax (FTT)* might lead to substantially higher trading costs in secondary markets and, therefore, to a deterioration of liquidity. This may reduce the demand for German Federal securities and increase the costs of issuance. b) *The LR as well as the NFSR requirements under Basel III* may have a negative impact on the demand for German Federal securities. The new requirements may restrict warehousing as well as market making. Additionally, these new requirements may have a negative impact on the Repo market and thus a negative impact on the functioning of the secondary market. c) *MiFID II/MiFIR requirements* could potentially make market making for German Federal securities a more challenging activity. This could result in wider bid-ask-spreads and increased market volatility.
Hungary	Currently, Hungary does not observe any major adverse impact on its primary market operations. However, *FTT* could significantly affect the sale of short term papers (T-Bills).
Iceland	Foreign exchange transactions have been subject to capital controls since the autumn of 2008. The Government of Iceland has presented to the Parliament legislation supporting a comprehensive strategy for the liberalisation of the capital account. The strategy is based on the fundamental principle that the controls must be lifted in stages without disrupting the economy and without imposing additional financial burdens on the Treasury. The introduction of a stability tax is part of the solution for dealing with the legacy of failed financial institutions. It is estimated that Treasury revenues from the stability tax could be up to 34% of GDP. With that in mind, the funding needs for the Treasury will decrease and, accordingly, affect the future issuance strategy.
Ireland	*Apart from FTT*, which looks most negative, Ireland assessed the impact of the following new regulations *not* in quantitative terms, but in *qualitative* terms concerning both Primary and Secondary Markets operations: *1) Volcker Rule:* The potential separation of "high-street" and "merchant-banking" functions will likely lead to a decrease in the pool of capital available for primary dealer market-making. Short-run, and viewed in isolation (ignoring any systemic benefits that may accrue on a global basis), this would diminish the appetite for inventory/position taking among the bulk of NTMA's market-makers. *2) Solvency II*: While initial estimates were that it would be positive for investment-grade bonds, at the expense of both equities and non-investment grade issuance an emerging concern Is that too much power may be handed to the rating agencies (and backward-looking risk models). This could lead to flows out of IGBs into higher-rated paper, based on considerations more of existing ratings and box-ticking than on prospective outlook. Insofar as data is available on the fund dispositions of Irish insurers at present, it might be hard to spot the difference that this would make. *3) Basel III:* The downstream impact of this is difficult to quantify but likely to have a negative impact on the ability of banks which act as primary dealers to dedicate capital to sovereigns. It may also impact the ability to hedge positions with these banks. *4) Shorting Restrictions*: No specific impact assessed. *5) FTT:* While primary issuance from sovereign issuers is to be exempt, the introduction of FTT in its current form is potentially catastrophic, on a systemic basis. Primary market issuance is heavily reliant on properly functioning liquid secondary markets. The level of tax proposed, along with the cascading effect will render current market making models uneconomic, leading to significant deterioration in market liquidity. In effect FTT seeks to raise revenues based on existing behaviour, and to simultaneously render this behaviour economically unfeasible. As proposed it would destroy private sector money transmission mechanisms, and force all money market transactions into the ECB and NCBs. *6) Swap Rules:* No direct adverse impact assessed for sovereign due to exemption from reporting and clearing especially with established 2-way collateral arrangements such as Ireland has in place – however this impact assessment may change depending on how the market adapts to the new regulations. *Other: MIFID II* - pre and post trade transparency: The concern from this regulation relates to how it will impact on liquidity in the sovereign bond market at a time when they are experiencing volatility wings and liquidity stresses.
Italy	New rules such as *Basel III, Solvency II, short sale restrictions, and the Volcker rule*, among others, are meant to reduce the occurrence of major financial instability episodes. On the other hand, there is little doubt that they may reduce the capability of the banking system to warehouse and distribute government bonds, in particular during the first stages of their implementation and when not adequately fine-tuned. In general, the impact of these new regulations will be mostly felt in terms of higher transaction costs in the secondary market for government bonds. However, these increased costs will inevitably spill-over into the primary markets, in terms of both higher borrowing costs and lower quality in the execution of the placement of bonds. *The Volcker rule* should provide for a special regime for market makers of government bonds so that credit institutions can trade in government securities for market making purposes and provide client services. *Mifid II* could lead to negative consequences at the level of the Regulatory Technical Standards, particularly concerning market making standards, the rules for disclosure before and after trading (pre and post-trading transparency), and the ratio of unexecuted orders to transactions. *The new CSD Regulation*, with its mandatory buy-ins, will have a likely impact on the pricing and market liquidity of European bond and repo markets.

Table 2.8. **Country-by-country overview of regulations with the largest (expected) impact on primary markets** *(cont.)*

	Country-by country overview
	The adverse impact of the Financial Transactions Tax (FTT) is likely to be significant, although its adverse impact is perhaps somewhat less severe in comparison to previous versions (it is now envisaged not to levy the tax directly on government bond trades). *The new rules that are designed to strengthen the credit risk management of swaps* may make the issuance of currency bonds (which usually require hedging of exchange rate risk) to be impossible, unless bilateral CSAs or CCP arrangements are in place.
Japan	Regarding Basel III, the Japanese authorities are monitoring closely the interest rate risk in the banking book (IRRBB).
Mexico	The Mexican financial system is characterised by a large presence of foreign banks. Around 70% of the resources intermediated by the banking sector is performed by foreign owned banks. Subsidiaries of U.S. banks control over a fifth of the Mexican banking system assets, while the subsidiaries of European G-SIBs (to which the ECP may be applied) control almost 50% per cent of the banking system assets. It is hard to exactly quantify the impact of new regulations mentioned in the survey. However, banking subsidiaries established in Mexico that will be subject to either, *the Volcker Rule* (VR), *the ECP*[1] or both have a market share of assets close to 70%. Since these new regulations will restrict their trading activities in Mexican securities, financing cost are likely to increase and liquidity will be reduced accordingly. *The impact of the ECP* on the Mexican financial system may be larger than the one stemming from the VR since the current ECP only excludes operations concerning sovereign securities of the European Union from proprietary trading restrictions but it fails to exempt operations of the banks' subsidiaries with their host country sovereigns (such as the Mexican government) as in the VR.[2] Regarding *Basel III*, changes in current banks' practices may tend to increase banks' capital requirements for sovereign exposures, which will increase the cost of issuing sovereign debt. In particular, global and local banks have been mostly applying zero *risk weights* to the sovereign debt of their own home-countries relying mostly on the guidance of their own supervisors. Global banks have also been applying lower risk weights to their subsidiaries' local-currency-denominated and funded sovereign exposures (following the Basel standardised approach). However, as a result of the regulatory consistency assessment programme (RCAP), many home country supervisors/global banks are starting to eliminate this favourable treatment to calculate the capital requirements for sovereign exposures from host countries in which their subsidiaries operate.
Netherlands	DSTA (the Dutch DMO) is closely monitoring all regulatory changes that could have an impact on our debt management operations. However, most of the new regulations have not yet been finalised. Therefore, it is hard to assess the potential (adverse) impact. Furthermore, it is difficult to assess whether certain regulatory changes will have a direct or indirect impact. Most EU directives will have an *indirect impact* since the funding operations by governments are exempt. One clear example of this indirect influence. The settlement time of government bonds changed from T+3 to T+2 due to the requirements of CSDR. Although DSTA is exempt, it was felt that the DMO could not lag behind the new market standard.
New Zealand	It is very difficult to isolate these regulatory changes and their impacts on issuance. New Zealand noted that regulation (more broadly) appears to be having an impact on liquidity and the ability of intermediaries to warehouse risk.
Norway	New regulations will probably have small effects.
Poland	The potential impact on primary markets from the *tax on financial transactions* (imposed in some EU-countries), is likely to manifest itself in a deterioration in the demand for government bonds. The *Volcker rule*, some provisions of *Basel III*, as well as *Regulation (EU) 236/2012 on short selling*, are likely to have an adverse effect on the market making capabilities of some of the primary dealers in the Polish market as well. This is likely to result in decreased liquidity and lower market depth, what may, in turn, impairs (to some degree) the price discovery process prior to primary auctions.
Portugal	*Volcker rule*: the absence of an exemption for European sovereign debt (similar to the one for US Treasuries or the securities issued by Fannie Mae and Freddie Mac) may shrink the investor base. All regulations that are having an adverse impact on secondary market transactions, are also having a potential negative influence on the primary market (in the form of higher funding costs and a smaller investor base).
Slovak Republic	Thus far, the Slovak authorities have not (yet) observed an (adverse) impact on the market from the new regulations.
Slovenia	*The financial transactions tax (FTT)*, as currently drafted, remains the greatest concern, because of its impact on secondary market liquidity, which, in turn, is expected to adversely influence primary market operations (higher borrowing costs; increased volatility of bid offer spreads). This is of great concern for Slovenia, as smaller and less liquid markets are expected to be more affected. *MIFID II and MIFIR* might impair the market making of government bonds and result in higher funding costs and lower liquidity (once again, especially for smaller markets).
Spain	*CRD-IV* restricts the amount of bonds that a PD can warehouse on its own balance sheet (due to increasing capital charges for volatile and lower-rated bonds). *The Financial Transactions Tax* could have a destructive effect on the execution of auctions (through an increase in secondary market volatility). *Volcker Rule* would affect Spanish banks mostly through the extraterritorial effects of the Dodd-Frank Act. *Solvency II* could have a positive effect on the demand for longer-duration Spanish public debt by certain types of buy-to-hold investors (pension funds, insurance companies).
Sweden	Most important is the indirect effect via the detrimental impact on the secondary market. But there may also be a direct effect on the primary market. For example, *MiFID II,MiFIR and Solvency II* reduce the demand for longer dated bonds.
Switzerland	In general, there is a lower risk appetite by banks (trading desk); proprietary trading has practically disappeared, and is now almost exclusively focused on customer flow. This increases price volatility and may widen bid/ask spread. However, there is continued demand by insurance companies for long and ultra-long dated government bonds.
Turkey	The impact of new regulations has two dimensions. On the one hand, new regulations in general involve restrictions on the execution of financial activities (e.g. lower liquidity, reduced mobility of capital and pressure on banks' profitability). On the other hand, there are positive effects in terms of sound risk management practices, a more stable investment environment and a stronger capital structure of banks. More specifically, *new rules on swaps* may constrain banks' ability to hedge their primary market operations. *Shorting restrictions* may cause short squeezes and adverse price movements, hence resulting in a deterioration of liquidity. *The Volcker Rule* is not expected to have an impact on Turkish primary markets. However, *Basel III, new rules for swaps and taxation* may have a strong effect.

Table 2.8. **Country-by-country overview of regulations with the largest (expected) impact on primary markets** *(cont.)*

	Country-by country overview
	Solvency II and Basel III may have an impact on CARs, while *shorting restrictions and new rules for swaps* may adversely affect liquidity. On the positive side, the introduction of the *liquidity coverage ratio (*LCR; part of Basel III) is likely to increase the appetite of banks for Treasury securities, either in primary markets or secondary markets.
United Kingdom	The DMO is very mindful of regulatory developments in Europe and internationally and realises that there are potentially significant impacts these can have on the sovereign debt markets. The DMO has a role in providing advice and analysis to HM Treasury on the implications of these regulatory initiatives, in particular for the gilt market, in order to ensure that any concerns for the gilt market/sovereign bonds are raised and given due consideration by the appropriate authorities. In addition, the UK DMO provides its view and participates in discussions on the impact of regulatory issues in various forums such as the EFC sub-committee on EU sovereign debt markets (ESDM) and other platforms for public sector borrowers. The performance of the DMO's issuance operations continues to remain sound. UK'DMO believe that this is in large part due to: i) the size, depth and liquidity of the gilt market; ii) the consequently relatively smooth adjustment of prices to allow supply to be taken down across maturities and types of gilts; and iii) competition between primary dealers that consequently offer fine pricing to investors. However, as regulatory initiatives begin to be implemented and/or become binding on primary dealers (e.g. *the Basel III disclosure requirements on leverage ratios* came into effect at the start of 2015 and apply to all firms; the *Volcker Rule* becomes binding for firms from July 2015), the consequences of regulation in the gilt market have begun to become more apparent. There have been recent indications of increased volatility in the gilt market as well as small changes in the bidding behaviour of primary dealers that could potentially reflect factors including the changing regulatory environment. It is very difficult to attribute these changes to specific pieces of regulation. Primary dealers have reported general concerns about the cumulative impact of regulation and the requirement for banks to hold more capital against assets including sovereign debt. Resulting balance sheet constraints could have the impact of a reduction in primary dealers' appetite for activities such as holding inventory, provision of liquidity and market making; all with a consequent impact on the primary market. Where specific regulatory initiatives have been mentioned, the *CRD IV regulation* (the leverage ratio in particular) has been noted by primary market participants to be the single most burdensome piece of regulation in terms of its capital requirements and subsequent impact on primary and secondary market activity. Other regulatory initiatives highlighted here are more likely to impact the secondary market which could have knock-on effects on the ability of the government to access the primary market and/or to do so in a cost effective manner.
United States	All else equal, *Basel III and derivatives clearing regulations* should increase demand for high-quality collateral. Accordingly, our primary market operations should see more competitive and/or increased investor participation. Conversely, although the *Volcker rule and proposed taxes on financial transactions* exempt new government issuance from its purview, the impact that these regulations will likely exert on our secondary market operations would adversely impact demand for our securities in the primary market.

1. The market share of assets from subsidiaries of European banks is around 50%.
2. Notice that while Mexican subsidiaries of American banks will be able to carry out operations with Mexican sovereign securities, American Banks established in the U.S. will not. The final version of the Volcker rule (VR) permits proprietary trading in foreign government obligations but with certain limitations.

Source: Responses to the 2015 survey on primary markets developments by the OECD Working Party on Public Debt Management.

always clear what the impact is of Basel III on primary market issuance but the adverse impact on market-making seems more evident. It may also impact the ability to hedge positions with primary dealer banks. The capital requirements and liquidity requirements of Basel III are causing dealers to hold more capital, which prevents them from cost effectively holding large amounts of securities and to act as principals in trades. As a result, investors are having a more difficult time to complete either side of a large trade.

It is very difficult to isolate all these regulatory changes and their impacts on issuance. Moreover, given the evolving nature of some of the regulatory changes, it is difficult to fully appreciate the impact that the new regulations will have on primary markets/operations in the debt management space.

Nonetheless, primary dealers have reported general concerns about the cumulative impact of regulation and the requirement for banks to hold more capital against assets including sovereign debt. Resulting balance sheet constraints could have the impact of a reduction in primary dealers' appetite for activities such as holding inventory, provision of liquidity and market making, all with a consequent impact on the primary market. Hence, the cumulative impact of regulation on sovereign debt markets is of crucial importance for sovereign issuers but, unfortunately, its quantification is not easy. However, it is clear that, in general, the new regulations are having (or will have) a significant influence on primary dealer banks and, as a result, public debt management operations. Banks will need to

Figure 2.1. **Largest (expected) impact of new regulations (in %) on the functioning of primary markets**

2015 Survey distribution answers*

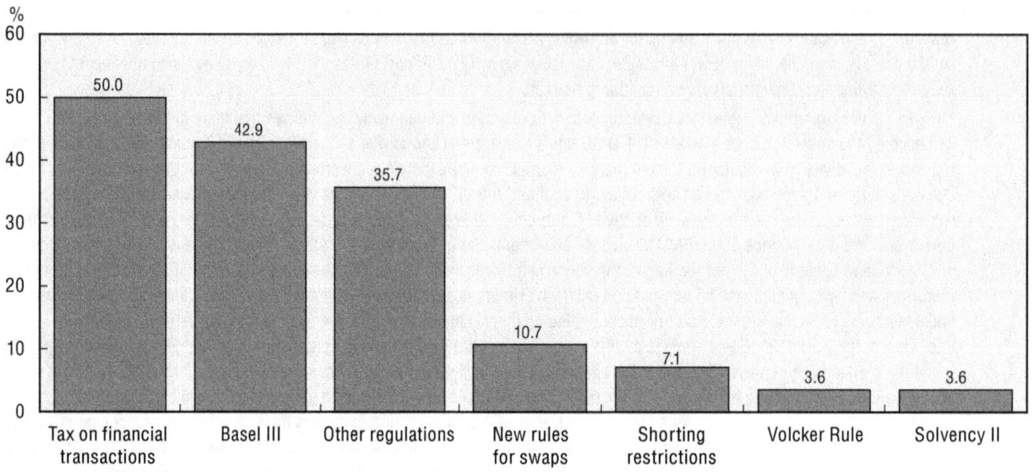

Regulation	%
Tax on financial transactions	50.0
Basel III	42.9
Other regulations	35.7
New rules for swaps	10.7
Shorting restrictions	7.1
Volcker Rule	3.6
Solvency II	3.6

* 28 OECD countries out of 34 answered this question. Note that respondents ranked more than one regulation with having the biggest (potential) impact on primary markets.

Source: Responses to the 2015 survey on primary markets developments by OECD Working Party on Debt Management.

StatLink http://dx.doi.org/10.1787/888933393173

adjust their business models (or are in the process of doing so) by excluding low-margin business areas which probably will affect in particular smaller, less liquid government bond markets. For example, the New Zealand DMO noted that regulation (more broadly) appears to be having an impact on liquidity and the ability of intermediaries to warehouse risk. But also in larger markets there may be an adverse impact. The Germany DMO reports that the liquidity in the cash market for German Federal securities (as well as in the repo and the futures markets) might decrease. As a result, activities in the primary market may become more challenging.

Finally, it was also noted that regulatory initiatives, either individually or cumulatively, have the potential to result in a number of *unintended* consequences (direct and indirect ones) for sovereign debt markets. For example, most of the countries in the survey also indicated that the Financial Transactions Tax (FTT) might lead to a substantial higher costs of secondary market trading and, hence, to a deterioration of market liquidity. It was reasoned that even while primary issuance from sovereign issuers is to be exempt, the introduction of FTT in its current form may have a major adverse impact on market liquidity. Primary market issuance is heavily reliant on properly functioning liquid secondary markets. The level of FTT proposed, along with the cascading effect, will render current market making models uneconomic, leading to significant deterioration in market liquidity. (See Chapter 3 for more details on liquidity in secondary markets for government bonds.).

Notes

1. Chapter 4 discusses details on the transparency of debt management strategies, policies and operations.
2. It is widely recognised that issuers, investors, dealers and tax payers have benefited from transparent, efficient, robust and reliable issuance procedures for government debt (Hans J. Blommestein [2002], editor, Debt Management and Government Securities Markets in the 21st Century, OECD).

3. At a multiple-price auction, bonds are sold at the actual bid price of successful bidders.
4. At a single-price (uniform-price or Dutch) auction, all bonds are sold at the same lowest accepted price.
5. "From an investor perspective, FRNs have less exposure to rising rates because of the frequent rate resets, and they pay interest more frequently than current coupon two-year securities. At the same time, FRNs may offer investors a slightly higher yield and fewer transaction costs than consistently rolling over a position in the thirteen-week bill, despite providing nearly identical cash flows." (See Copic, E., L. Gonzalez, C. Gorback, B. Gwinn and E. Schaumburg (2014), "Introduction to the Floating-Rate Note Treasury Security", *Liberty Street Economics*, 21 April.)
6. A "Schuldschein" is a loan instrument usually governed by German law, and sometimes translated as a "certificate of indebtedness". A "Schuldschein" is a bilateral loan, privately placed, unlisted and unregistered. They are not securities as the debt is legally constituted by the underlying loan agreement, rather than by the certificate of indebtedness itself. Historically, the largest category of issuers of a "Schuldschein" has been German public authorities, although the market has also been tapped by other borrowers.

Chapter 3

Liquidity in secondary markets for government bonds

This chapter discusses changes in liquidity in secondary government bond markets. Debt managers (and market participants) have expressed concerns that some of the regulatory changes in response to the global financial crisis may have an adverse (direct) impact on liquidity in secondary markets for government bonds. Debt Management Offices (DMOs) argue that lower liquidity in these markets is likely to affect primary market issuance in the form of a rise in borrowing cost.

The statistical data for Israel are supplied by and under the responsibility of the relevant Israeli authorities. The use of such data by the OECD is without prejudice to the status of the Golan Heights, East Jerusalem and Israeli settlements in the West Bank under the terms of international law.

3.1. Introduction

Secondary market liquidity is an essential feature of a well-functioning and resilient government bond market. Investors and traders place a high value on being able to trade sizeable volumes of bonds without the risk that these trades will impact on bond prices. Liquidity in government bond markets also has a direct impact on funding possibilities and financing costs. Moreover, liquid government bond markets support the development of financial markets more generally, because of the important benchmark or reference role played by marketable government debt.

This chapter* on liquidity in secondary government bond markets contains policy information based on a Survey among debt managers from the OECD Working Party on Debt Management (WPDM) (see ANNEX). As of 31 October 2015, 30 members of the WPDM out of 34 replied to the survey.[1]

Key findings

- Since the onset of the global financial crisis, many (new) factors had an (adverse) impact on the liquidity of government bond markets. Some of these relate to quantitative easing (QE), others to regulatory changes. Liquidity conditions in surveyed countries vary for foreign and local issuances, and depending on composition holders, trading practices and market infrastructures.
- DMOs have taken additional measures to boost liquidity. These actions include buy backs of illiquid lines, larger benchmark lines, a strips programme, the use of a lender of last resort facility, etc. Also, DMOs support liquidity by implementing predictable and transparent policies.
- The ongoing process of regulatory changes in the financial system (Basel III, Solvency II, CACs, MiFID II, Dodd-Frank Act, etc.) will probably have (or is having) an impact on secondary market liquidity of government bonds. For example, trading in government bonds has become increasingly challenging amid dealers' balance sheet constraints due to increased capital requirements for banks.

3.2. Liquidity of foreign currency bonds versus domestic currency bonds

The responses show that 16 OECD DMOs out of 30 responding countries (55%) report that the relative liquidity of foreign currency bonds (in comparison to domestic currency bonds) is lower (Figure 3.1), while 1 DMO argues that it is higher. Two DMOs note that foreign currency bonds and domestic currency bonds have similar bid-ask spreads. Eight OECD countries (28%) do not issue foreign currency bonds.[2]

* Chapter written by Hans J. Blommestein with research and statistical support by Perla Ibarlucea Flores. Tables and figures are based on responses to the 2015 survey on "liquidity in secondary markets for government bonds" by the OECD WPDM (cut-off date 31 October, 2015).

Figure 3.1. **Liquidity of foreign currency bonds in comparison to domestic currency bonds**

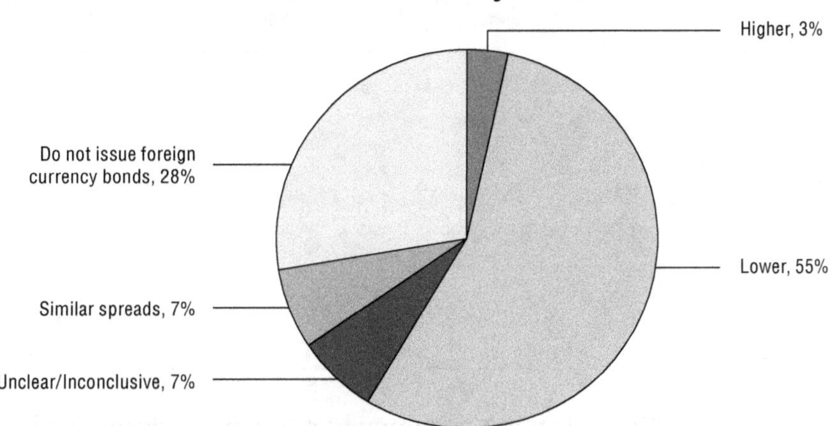

Note: 29 out of 30 responding countries answered this question.
Source: Responses to the 2015 survey on liquidity in secondary markets for governments bonds by OECD Working Party on Debt Management.

StatLink http://dx.doi.org/10.1787/888933393186

Table 3.1 shows that the reasons for lower liquidity in foreign currency bonds include the use of a different issuance strategy. For example, the country notes to Table 3.1 for Belgium and the Netherlands indicate that the strategy related to the issuance of domestic bonds is focused on liquidity, predictability and transparency, while the strategy for foreign currency bonds is focused on cost efficiency and investor diversification.

Table 3.1. **Liquidity of foreign currency bonds versus domestic bonds**

	Higher	Lower	Unclear/Inconclusive	Similar spreads	Do not issue foreign currency bonds
Australia					X
Austria				X	
Belgium		X			
Canada		X			
Chile				X	
Czech Republic		X			
Denmark		X			
Finland		X			
France					X
Germany		X			
Greece					
Hungary		X			
Iceland		X			
Ireland					X
Israel		X			
Italy		X			
Japan					X
Korea		X			
Luxembourg					X
Mexico		X			
Netherlands		X			
New Zealand					X
Norway					X
Poland			X		

Table 3.1. Liquidity of foreign currency bonds versus domestic bonds (*cont.*)

	Higher	Lower	Unclear/Inconclusive	Similar spreads	Do not issue foreign currency bonds
Portugal		X			
Slovak Republic					
Slovenia			X		
Spain		X			
Sweden					
Switzerland					X
Turkey	X				
United Kingdom		X			
United States					
Total	1	16	2	2	8

Table 3.1. Liquidity of foreign currency bonds versus domestic bonds (continuation with country notes)

Austria	Foreign currency bonds trade at similar or slightly wider bid/ask spreads compared to domestic currency bonds (although indicated and traded volumes are lower).
Belgium	The liquidity of Belgium's foreign currency bonds (as well as EMTNs in EUR and retail bonds) is lower than the liquidity of Belgium's OLOs (Linear Bonds) because of different issuing strategies. The strategy related to the issuance of OLOs is focused on liquidity, predictability and transparency, while the strategy for foreign currency bonds (and EMTNs and retail bonds in general) is focused on cost efficiency and investor diversification. The joint lead managers in Belgium's foreign currency bonds do provide liquidity but they do not have to meet the same sort of obligations as those exist for domestic bonds.
Canada	Generally, the liquidity of foreign currency bonds is lower than that of Government of Canada domestic-currency bonds, as global bonds are issued less frequently and have smaller outstanding amounts. In addition, a large proportion of global bond issuances is held by buy-and-hold investors such as central banks, making global bonds less liquid than domestic bonds.
Chile	In terms of bid-ask spreads, the liquidity has been similar in both market segments.
Czech Republic	Due to the existence of a dedicated secondary market trading platform (MTS), domestic Czech Republic bonds are much more liquid than bonds issued in foreign currency.
Denmark	Under normal circumstances domestic bonds are more liquid than foreign currency bonds. The domestic funding rule states that the central government should borrow in Danish kroner to cover its financing requirements. Hence, the market for domestic bonds is much larger than for foreign bonds. In addition, a primary dealer system with price quoting obligations is in place regarding domestic bonds, thereby further supporting liquidity. Foreign bonds are typically issued through syndications. This can result in a smaller turnover for foreign currency bonds than those issued in domestic currency.
Finland	Foreign currency bonds are less liquid, because no quoting obligations exits similar to those for EUR benchmark bonds.
France	France has not issued foreign currency bonds.
Germany	Currently, Germany is not issuing foreign currency bonds. However, to date, two USD bonds with maturities of three and five years have been issued by Germany (the latter matured in 2012). As a rule, the liquidity of Germany's foreign currency bonds is lower than those of domestic bonds.
Hungary	The liquidity of Hungarian domestic bonds is clearly much better due to the greater number of lines, the market making structure with price quotations by primary dealers, and regular issuances.
Iceland	Icelandic foreign currency issues are much less liquid than domestic bonds.
Israel	Domestic bonds are more liquid than foreign currency bonds.
Italy	Domestic bonds are much more liquid than foreign currency bonds issued in the Global Bond or the MTN format. Foreign bonds normally benefit from a certain degree of liquidity for just a few months after issuance. In recent years, Italy has not issued foreign currency bonds.
Korea	Liquidity of domestic bonds is much higher than of foreign currency bonds.
Mexico	The liquidity of local currency bonds is higher than the liquidity of foreign currency bonds. This can be explained by several factors: 1) Outstanding amount: the outstanding amount of domestic-currency debt is more than 6 times than the outstanding amount of foreign-currency debt. The average issued amount of domestic bonds (MBonds and Udibonos) is approximately USD 7.8 billion while the average issued amount of foreign-currency bonds is USD 1.5 billion. 2) Diversified investor base for domestic bonds: about 45% of the issued amount of MBonds and Udibonos is held by foreign investors (i.e. hedge funds, mutual funds, banks, private pension funds, among others), while 26% is held by local pension funds. The rest is in hands of local banks, brokerage houses, insurance companies and treasuries. 3) A good system for Market-Making is in place. This MM system provides liquidity in the secondary market (every financial institution that acts as Market Maker is required to quote bid/ask rates on a daily basis for every line of

Table 3.1. **Liquidity of foreign currency bonds versus domestic bonds (continuation with country notes)**

	outstanding domestic bonds). 4) Inclusion in global indices: The inclusion of domestic debt in several international indices has given greater depth to the government securities market. Particularly, after the inclusion of MBonds to the WGBI in 2010, foreign holdings in these instruments have registered a significant increase (for example, in October 2010, foreign investor held 29% of the total issued amount of MBonds, while in June 2015 this share had increased to 59%). It is important to note that the strategic objective of public debt management is to finance the needs of the Federal Government mainly through domestic borrowing operations (so as to maintain a debt structure in which liabilities are predominantly denominated in local currency). The Federal Government has maintained access to international markets
Netherlands	The liquidity of foreign currency bonds issued by the Dutch government is relatively limited. Whereas the DMO is committed to establish and maintain a liquid and complete yield curve for domestic currency bonds up to ten years, this is not the case for USD bonds which are issued by the Netherlands more opportunistically.
Poland	The foreign bonds issued by the State Treasury are registered on foreign stock exchanges. However, the trading of those securities is concentrated on non- (or lightly) regulated interbank markets that are characterised by a significant degree of decentralisation and also by a large number of institutions actively participating in transactions. Those features of the interbank market make it difficult to supervise trading transactions; in practice, the only bond parameter that can be observed and can be used to describe a bond's performance is the spread above benchmark yields. Bonds issued in Euro as well as US dollar markets are fairly liquid. This is mainly due to the depth of both markets and the size of transactions (issues of nominal bonds are not less than 1 billion). In the case of Swiss franc bonds and Samurai (acting as so-called supplementary markets) the situation is different because the size of bond issues is significantly smaller. Hence, liquidity is low(er). The liquidity of domestic bonds can be assessed as quite satisfactory. The liquidity ratio, calculated as the ratio of the average value of transactions to the average amount of all outstanding bonds, remained fairly stable during the last two years at around 180%. The most liquid bonds are 2-, 5- and 10-year benchmarks. Their average liquidity ratios amounted to 221%, 356% and 344% respectively.
Portugal	The liquidity of foreign bonds should be much smaller than those of domestic benchmark bonds, considering, on the one hand, the smaller size and more concentrated ownership of foreign bonds and, on the other, the primary dealer requirements for domestic benchmarks.
Slovenia	The liquidity of domestic currency bonds which meet the MTS Slovenia selection criteria (1.0 billion EUR/USD 1.08 billion in nominal value) is being supported by the daily market obligation of the Primary Dealers. Moreover, there is no interbank market for foreign (USD) bonds. (The liquidity of USD deals is based on OTC, Bloomberg trading.) The priority of banks is to maintain liquidity of the B2C market. In addition, the primary dealer system (established only for domestic currency government bonds), involves the obligation of primary dealers (PDs): 1) to contribute to the liquidity of the government bonds in secondary market segments and 2) to report on a monthly basis on their trading activity using the new European harmonised reporting format. (The performance of PDs is measured by a Performance Index which includes the evaluation of their secondary market trading activity.) In contrast, there is no market-making (primary dealer) framework for foreign currency bonds. (This makes also the issuer's access to information on foreign currency government bond liquidity more difficult.) Hence, due to the structural differences in the set-up of primary and secondary markets for domestic and foreign currency bonds, a comparison of the liquidity in these two secondary market segments is less straightforward.
Spain	The liquidity of foreign bonds is significantly lower than of domestic bonds due to smaller issues and less frequent issuance and also the absence of obligations for PDs to make markets.
Turkey	Recently, the liquidity of Turkish domestic bonds has decreased significantly. This negative trend was less pronounced in international markets. Hence, it could be argued that foreign currency bonds are more liquid than domestic bonds.
United Kingdom	The UK government continues to meet its domestic financing requirements entirely in sterling via the gilt market, which is deemed to be liquid in general. The comparatively very small amount raised by the issuance of the Renminbi bond was used to finance the UK government's reserves of foreign currency. Given the very small size and currency of the issue, the bond is highly unlikely to be liquid.

Note:

1. Italy: by definition, most of the foreign currency bonds issued in the MTN format are non-liquid, as they are issued in a reverse enquiry transaction and, normally, held to maturity by the institutional investor for which they are tailored.
2. Estonia has no outstanding government bonds; the debt portfolio of the State Treasury consists entirely of a loan from the EIB.
3. Japan, New Zealand, Ireland, Australia, Luxembourg, Norway and Switzerland have not issued (or are not issuing) foreign-currency bonds.

Source: Responses to the 2015 survey on liquidity in secondary markets for governments bonds by OECD Working Party on Debt Management.

Other explanations given by DMOs for the lower liquidity of foreign bonds are that they are issued less frequently with smaller outstanding amounts (see Canada in Table 3.1) and also a relatively narrow investor base (see Mexico in Table 3.1). Note in this context that the strategic objective of public debt management of many governments is to finance the needs of the central government mainly through domestic borrowing operations (so as to maintain a debt structure in which liabilities are predominantly denominated in local currency).

DMOs also point to the importance of having in place a good system for market-making (by primary dealers) and the inclusion of domestic (currency) debt in global indices (see Mexico in Table 3.1).

However, some DMOs (see Slovenia in Table 3.1) argue that due to the structural differences in the set-up of primary and secondary markets for domestic and foreign currency bonds, a comparison of the liquidity in these two secondary market segments is less straightforward.

3.3. Structure of secondary government securities markets

Table 3.2 provides key information on the structure of secondary government securities markets by reporting or calculating the following characteristics i) the total number of domestic lines for sovereign bonds (and Treasury bills); ii) the different types of domestic lines (nominal fixed-rate bonds, inflation-indexed bonds, floaters, retail bonds, zero coupon bonds); and iii) indicators for the size of bond lines on issue. Figure 3.3 provides additional information in terms of the percentage of bonds held domestically versus those held offshore.

The first defining characteristic is the total number of lines. This market feature differs greatly across markets with the number of domestic currency government bond (and Treasury bill) lines ranging from Luxembourg with 6 lines to Italy with 115 lines (Table 3.2).

Also the diversity of instruments issued by DMOs is considerable, although many DMOs sell both nominal fixed-rate bonds and inflation-indexed bonds. This diversity feature probably reflects the size of borrowing requirements and the associated need to create a relatively wide investor base.

The average number of bond lines between USD 5 billion and USD 10 billion on issue is about 19 lines. Italy and France have the largest number of bond lines of this size, with 113 and 83, respectively.

Issuance size is usually a necessary (but not sufficient) condition for liquid markets. For example, the average number of bond lines greater that USD 10 billion on issue is about 14 lines of domestic currency bonds (including treasury bills for certain countries). Italy, France and United Kingdom have the largest number of bond lines of this size, with 57, 93 and 65 respectively. Moreover, there are issuers like Germany, Netherlands and Japan with only bond lines on issue greater than USD 10 billion (see Figure 3.2).

It can also be deduced from Table 3.2 and Figure 3.2 that the following countries have domestic currency bond lines lower that USD 5 billion on issue: Slovak Republic, Slovenia, Chile, Czech Republic, Hungary, Iceland and Luxembourg.

Figure 3.3 provides additional information on the structure of secondary government securities markets in terms of the percentage of bonds held domestically versus those held offshore. The diversity is striking. In Japan and Israel, domestic holdings are more than 90%. In Germany and Finland, domestic holdings are 15% or lower. In the Netherlands, domestic holdings are around the average percentage of bonds held domestically of 50%.

Table 3.2. **Structure of secondary government bond markets**

	Number of domestic currency bond lines	Number of bond lines greater than USD 5 billion on issue	Number of bond lines greater than USD 10 billion on issue
Australia	28 domestic currency bonds (of which 21 Treasury Bonds and 7 Treasury Indexed Bonds [linkers]).	19	14
Austria	22 domestic currency bond lines.	18	7
Belgium	27 domestic currency bond lines.	24	19
Canada	51 outstanding Government of Canada Marketable bonds payable in domestic currency (including inflation adjustments for real return bonds).	43	28
Chile	12 domestic currency bond lines.	0	0
Czech Republic	41 domestic currency bond lines (including 18 saving bond lines).	0	0
Denmark	13 domestic currency bond lines (of which 10 nominal bonds, 1 index linked bonds and 2 Treasury bills).	9	5
Finland	Currently there are 15 benchmark bond lines.	13	0
France	There are currently 90 lines (66 excluding bills).	83	57
Germany	10 domestic currency lines of which 2 Bubills lines (money market instruments) and 8 bond lines (capital market instruments).	0	7
Hungary	22 bond lines (of which 17 fixed-rate bonds and 5 floating-rate bonds; excluding retail and private placement bonds).	0	0
Iceland	12 domestic currency bond lines.	0	0
Ireland	32 domestic currency bond lines.	15	3
Israel	31 domestic currency bond lines.	1	0
Italy	115 domestic currency lines (of which 19 lines of bills, 63 lines of bonds, 11 lines of floaters, 10 lines of indexed inflation linker, 4 lines of zero coupon bonds and 8 lines of retail bonds).	113	93
Japan	12 domestic currency bond lines.	0	12
Korea	Domestic currency bonds can be divided into three types: i) Korea Treasury Bonds, ii) Treasury Bills, and iii) National Household Bonds. As for Korean Treasury Bonds, there are 44 bond lines (of which 39 fixed bonds, and 5 inflation-indexed bonds).	34	24
Luxembourg	6 domestic currency bond lines.	0	0
Mexico	There are 29 bond lines of which 20 issued Mbonds (Nominal Fixed-Rate Bonds) and 9 issued Udibonos (Inflation-Linked Bonds).	20	5
Netherlands	There are 24 domestic currency bond lines. In addition, there are 3 perpetuals outstanding, but the outstanding amounts are very small (in total less than € 15 million).	0	24
New Zealand	There are currently 10 domestic currency bond lines.	4	0
Norway	There are currently 6 domestic currency bond lines.	5	0
Poland	There are currently 30 domestic currency bond lines.	17	0
Portugal	There are currently 20 domestic currency bond lines.	11	4
Slovak Republic	There are currently 19 domestic currency bond lines.	0	0
Slovenia	There are currently 19 domestic currency government bonds.	0	0
Spain	There are 45 lines of domestic coupon bonds of which 3 lines linked to the Euro Area Harmonised Index Consumer Price HICP (excluding Tobacco). In addition, there are 12 lines of zero-coupon bills.	42	35
Switzerland	There are currently 22 domestic currency bond lines outstanding.	5	0
United Kingdom	There are currently 41 nominal lines and 25 inflation-linked.	66	65
	Average number of domestic currency bond lines	19	14

Note: Estonia has no outstanding government bonds; the debt portfolio of the State Treasury consists entirely of a loan from the EIB.
Source: 2015 Survey on liquidity in secondary government bond markets by OECD Working Party on Debt Management.

For Eurozone countries there is some discussion whether (and to which extent) the Eurozone should be treated as a domestic market (the Euro is the domestic currency of both the issuer and many investors). For example, in Austria the share of domestic holdings is around 25%. This share would increase to around 80% when the whole Eurozone is considered as the domestic market.

Figure 3.2. **Number of domestic currency bond lines by country**

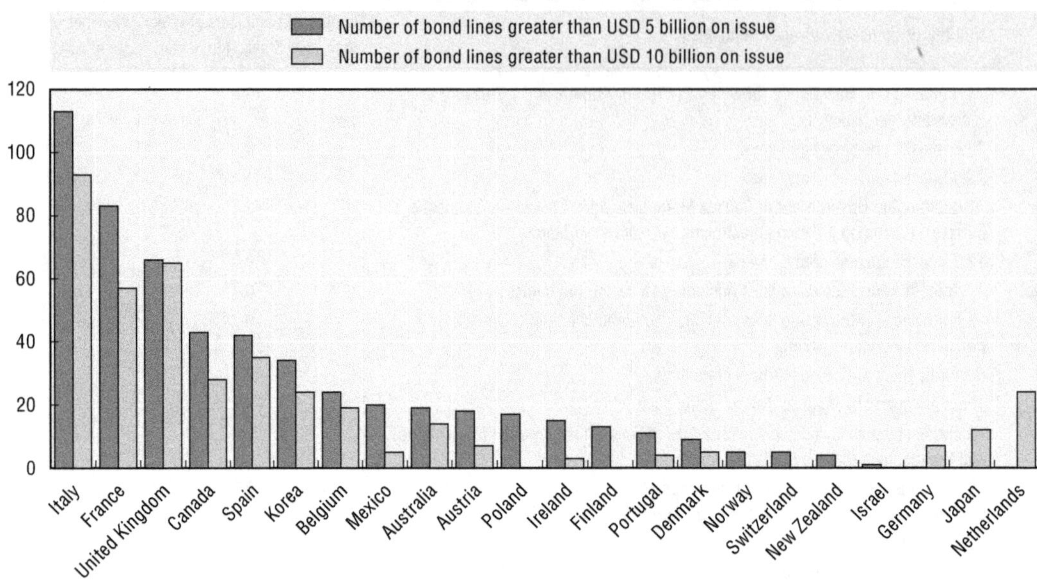

Source: 2015 Survey on liquidity in secondary government bond markets by OECD Working Party on Debt Management.

StatLink http://dx.doi.org/10.1787/888933393197

3.4. Trading practices for government bonds

This section discusses the trading practices for government bonds by using three indicators: i) standard market parcel size for trades in government bonds; ii) proportion of secondary market trades conducted via voice and iii) proportion of secondary market trades conducted electronically (see Table 3.3).

The standard market parcel size varies significantly across markets, ranging from USD 760 000 in Iceland to USD 80 million for brokers in the UK. Debt managers reported that the parcel size may vary depending on maturity and/or type of market participant (broker or client) (see UK in Table 3.3). The Table also shows that minimum and maximum sizes differ considerably. It was also noted that the market parcel size for trades in government bonds saw an increase after the ECB initiated QE operations (see Slovak Republic in Table 3.3).

The proportion of secondary market trades conducted via voice across markets differs markedly. There is a wide range from 0% in Israel to 91-98% in Hungary and Poland. This also implies that the proportion of secondary market trades conducted electronically shows a similar variation across national (domestic) trades.

The proportion of trades conducted electronically shows an increase over time (although some of this information is anecdotal). For example, Italy notes that, based on information provided by Italy's Primary Dealers, voice trades have decreased. Some governments report that they encourage electronic trading (for example, the Czech Republic).

There can also be complex links between electronic platforms and voice contacts. For example, New Zealand reports that secondary market trades are still predominantly voice-based but that electronic platforms are beginning to evolve that are used to indicate pricing in order to initiate voice contact.

Figure 3.3. **Percentage of bonds held domestically vs. offshore**

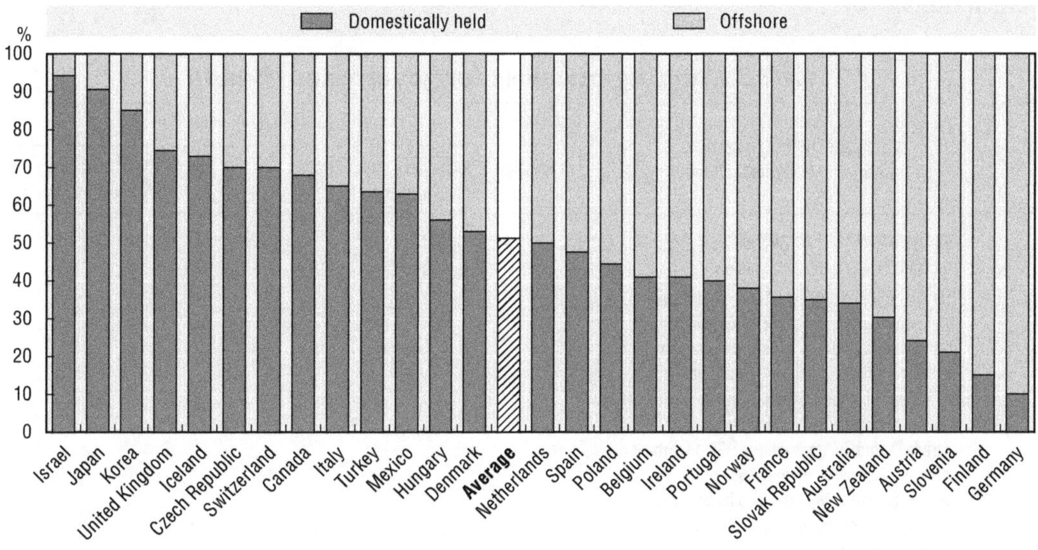

Note: 26 countries provided information as of 30 June 2015.

1. Australia, Canada, France, Japan and United Kingdom as of 31 March 2015. Ireland as of 30 April 2015. Portugal and Switzerland as of 31 May 2015.
2. When the Eurozone is treated as the domestic market the share of domestically held bonds would be 80% in Austria.
3. For Belgium, 41% is held domestically vs. 59% abroad (of which 32% in the Eurozone; the domestic currency of the issuer and investors).
4. As of May 2015, 32% of domestic Canadian government bonds were held by non-residents. Global bonds are sold to offshore investors; information is not available to determine whether some domestic investors have obtained these bonds in the secondary market.
5. For the Czech Republic, approximately 30% of government securities (T-bonds and T-bills) are held offshore, assuming that the foreign-currency bonds are held solely by non-residents. (However, the Ministry of Finance has no information about these foreign holdings)
6. Regarding Finland, it is estimated that around 15% is held domestically and 85% outside Finland. (However, a large part of the latter is held in the Eurozone – i.e. the domestic currency of the issuer and investors.)
7. For Hungary, domestic vs. offshore ownership of HUF bonds is 56 vs 44 per cent; in case of foreign currency bonds it is 17 vs 83 per cent (excluding retail papers).
8. In the case of Japan, foreign investors hold just below 10% of outstanding JGBs (this includes Treasury Discount Bills).
9. The Netherlands Statistical Bureau estimated in June 2015 that approximately 50% of domestic currency bonds are held domestically.
10. The Banco de Portugal estimated that in May 2015, 60% of outstanding tradable medium- and long-term sovereign bonds were held offshore (including ECB SMP programme holdings).
11. For the case of Spain, 52.39% of registered holdings of Non-stripped Bonos and Obligaciones are held by non-residents (47.61% is held domestically). Registered holdings include securities held as collateral in bilateral repo operations. In the case of Principal-Only Strips: 17.76% of the registered holdings are held by non-residents (82.24% is held domestically). In the case of Interest-Only Strips 19.01% of registered holdings are held by non-residents (80.99% held domestically).
12. According to data based on surveys by the Swiss National Bank, as of May 2015, approximately 30% of Switzerland bonds are held by foreign investors (at the end of 2014 this was 26%).
13. For the case of Turkey, 19.2% of the total domestic currency debt stock is held by non-residents. 70% of the total foreign currency debt stock is held by non-residents.
14. For United Kingdom, as of 31 March 2015, holdings are split as follows: overseas holders 25.5%, domestic investors 49.8% and Bank of England 24.8% (note: figures do not sum to 100% due to rounding).

Source: Responses to the 2015 survey on liquidity in secondary markets for governments bonds by OECD the Working Party on Debt Management.

StatLink http://dx.doi.org/10.1787/888933393208

The reasons why traders are trading outside organised market places (OTC) are important for explaining the proportion of trades conducted via voice. It may also be important to take into account the size of secondary market trades. For example, the UK observes that e-trading is more common for smaller-sized transactions. Also Belgium notes that larger tickets tend to be executed by voice rather than conducted electronically.

Hence the proportion of trades conducted electronically will be higher for smaller transactions.

Table 3.3. **Trading practices for government bonds**

	Standard market parcel size for trades in government bonds[1]	Trading practices	
		Proportion of secondary market trades conducted via voice, %	Proportion of secondary market trades conducted electronically, %
Australia	Approximately USD 15-20 million.	30	70
Austria	Standard size is USD 27.8 million.	40	60
Belgium	The average size traded on the most liquid inter-dealer platform is USD 9.6 million, but this conceals a variety of tickets between USD 1.1 and 55.5 million. Overall, in terms of number of trades, the distribution is heavily skewed towards smaller-sized trades. In terms of traded volumes, transactions USD 11.1 million and more represent almost 75% of the secondary traded volume. The larger tickets tend to be executed by voice rather than over an electronic platform.	20	80
Canada	Standard ticket size is USD 40.03 million.	50	50
Chile	Standard ticket size is USD 19.685 million for inflation linked bonds and USD 7.879 million for bonds in pesos.	It can be inferred from information on transactions of Treasury securities that at least 30% are conducted electronically.	
Czech Republic	Standard ticket size is USD 2.1 million.	The DMO reports that reliable data is not available. However, electronic and voice trading seem to be balanced. The Czech Republic encourages electronic trading.	
Denmark	The standard market parcel size depends on the type of bond. For government bonds, the typical parcel size is between 3 and 15 million USD.	The majority of Danish government securities are still traded outside organised marketplaces (as over-the-counter transactions or OTC). In 2014, approximately 75 per cent of trades was OTC.	
Finland	The standard ticket size is USD 10 million.	35	65
France	Standard clip is USD 10 million, but a significant number of transactions have a size higher than USD 50 million and account for most of the total volume traded.	70	30
Germany	Overall, more than USD 23.7 billion in bonds are traded every day. The average ticket size is about USD 9.3 Million (in 2015).	Information is not available.	
Hungary	The volume of benchmark bonds for which PDs quote obligatory prices is USD 1.8 million.	98	2
Iceland	The standard ticket size is USD 760 000.	1	99
Ireland	The standard ticket size is approximately USD 1-6 million.	The majority of trades, estimated at 60%, are executed via voice.	
Israel	Use of MTS trading platform. For bonds falling under the quoting obligation, the minimum quote size is 10 million in nominal value. For the 10 year benchmark bond (which currently trades at around 96.2) the usual trade size is around ILS 9.62 million or about USD 2.46 million.	0	100
Italy	On MTS (the electronic fixed income trading platform) the lots are at least 0.5 million euro or a multiple thereof.	Since 2013, voice trades have decreased to around 35% (as measured by the average of trading volumes in the period from January 2014 to 30 June 2015; this information is based on data collected by using the harmonised reporting format for Italy's Primary Dealers).	
Japan	Information is not available.	Information is not available.	

Table 3.3. **Trading practices for government bonds** *(cont.)*

	Standard market parcel size for trades in government bonds[1]	Trading practices	
		Proportion of secondary market trades conducted via voice, %	Proportion of secondary market trades conducted electronically, %
Korea	In the secondary KRX bond market, primary dealers are trading in multiple amounts of KRW 1 billion (or around USD 0.9 million). In the OTC market this amount is about KRW 10 billion (or around USD 9 million).	Trades on the KRX bond market are conducted electronically. The KRX bond market accounts for 50-55 percent of the total volume of bonds being traded.	
Luxembourg	Information is not available.	Information is not available.	
Mexico	During the last 5 years, the average trading amount per transaction for both MBonds and Udibonos is USD 1.8 million.	66.3	33.7
Netherlands	Information is not available.	Information is not available.	
New Zealand	Standard minimum market parcel for prices with the brokers is NZD 5 m however actual prices more regularly NZD 10 m. Actual dealt parcels normally larger that this if prices executed. Volumes are largely unchanged over the past five years with actual traded volume a function of underlying customer flows being absorbed through the market. Periods of volatility will result in pockets in which less volume trades and liquidity in general seems scarce. Price transparency during these periods can be difficult	Secondary market trades are still predominantly voice based. These would be either client to dealer; or, dealer to dealer vis a voice broker. Electronic platforms are beginning to evolve by to date are used to indicate pricing in order to initiate voice contact	
Norway	Standard size is USD 13 million	Information is not available.	
Poland	1) Average of PLN 14.9 m (USD 3.9 m) on Treasury BondSpot platform (dedicated electronic market for government bonds – using the MTS technology); the minimum value of a single transaction is PLN 5 m (USD 1.3 m). 2) Average of PLN 23.7 bn (USD 6.3 bn) on the OTC market (with Primary Dealers as participants; data based on the monthly reports submitted by PDs).	Trading on domestic T-bonds is mostly done on the OTC market: 91-96% of trades versus 4-7% on the electronic platform (Treasury BondSpot Poland).	
Portugal	On the intra-dealer platforms the average trade size is USD 7.2 million. The average size of OTC trades is USD 4.2 million (according to HRF reports).	49.64	50.36
Slovak Republic	There is no standard size. The average market parcel size for trades was 5.8 million USD in May 2015 (based on Bratislava Stock exchange data). Primary dealers reports trade sizes ranging from 555 000 to 5.5 million USD (with average size of around 1.1 million USD). After the ECB introduced QE, some tickets were 11.1 million USD or larger.	There is no dedicated electronic platform for Slovak bonds. PDs are reporting the following. 1) Domestic PDs report that almost 100% of the trades are electronically (Bloomberg ALLQ). 2) Non-domestic PDs report a growing share of trades done electronically but that the share of voice is still slightly more than 50%.	
Slovenia	On MTS Slovenia, the *minimum* size trade is USD 1.12 million, while the *average* trade size is USD 1.34 million. On LJSE (the securities exchange), the minimum and average trade size is less than USD 0.11 million.	30	70
Spain	For outright trades, both between account holders and with third parties, the average trade size for Bonos & Obligaciones is USD 11 million (average calculated as total volume of transactions divided by the number of transactions). The average for Letras del Tesoro is USD 19 million.	76	24

Table 3.3. **Trading practices for government bonds** *(cont.)*

	Standard market parcel size for trades in government bonds[1]	Trading practices	
		Proportion of secondary market trades conducted via voice, %	Proportion of secondary market trades conducted electronically, %
Switzerland	The average size of a transaction is USD 1.8 million; the minimum size is USD one million, the maximum size is up to USD 300-400 million.	Information is not available. However, regarding the average size of a transaction of Swiss government bonds, the DMO assumes that the majority of secondary market trades is conducted via voice.	
Turkey	In the period January-June 2015, the average trade volume (nominal value) is 1 003 163 TRY. The median size is 300 000 TRY, while the mode is 100 000 TRY. These values are based on outright purchases and sales on the Istanbul Debt Securities Market (part of the securities exchange – the Borsa).		
United Kingdom	Depending on maturity this ranges between GBP 5-50mn (USD 8-80 million) for brokers and between GBP 5-25 mn (USD 8-40 million) for clients.	Although this is not definitively known, anecdotal evidence suggests around 35% voice, 65% electronic for total volumes traded; e-trading is more common for smaller-sized transactions, hence the percentage for number of transactions will be higher here (circa 90% are electronic tickets by number).	

1. Information in millions of USD as of 30 June 2015.
Source: 2015 Survey on liquidity in secondary government bond markets by the OECD Working Party on Debt Management.

3.5. Liquidity of domestic sovereign bonds versus non-sovereign bonds issued in the domestic currency market

DMOs were also requested to evaluate the liquidity of their sovereign local currency bonds versus the liquidity of non-sovereign domestic currency bonds.

Twenty-six OECD DMOs out of 30 opined that their sovereign domestic currency bonds are definitely more liquid than other (non-sovereign) local currency bonds. Domestic sovereign bonds are normally more liquid than other issuers in the domestic market, having the largest bond programme, the largest amount on issue and the lowest borrowing costs of domestic issuers. Moreover, government bond markets serve in most cases as an important benchmark for other domestic issuers across the curve. Even in situations where exact or accurate figures for turnover ratios, daily trading volumes or spreads are not available, DMOs judged that sovereign bonds are far more liquid than corporate bonds. However, some non-sovereign bond markets are fairly liquid. For example, studies show that the liquidity of Danish mortgage bonds is quite similar to Danish government bonds. Also the bonds issued by two major Swiss Pfandbriefe institutions are quite liquid. In fact, Swiss bond traders judge mortgage bonds as more liquid than the Confederation bonds.

Even in markets where sovereign bonds are not highly liquid, demand is strong. This enables the construction of the local yield curve (see Table 3.4) which market players use as pricing reference.

Other (non-sovereign) issuers in the domestic currency market are often much smaller and cannot provide the same liquidity as sovereign issuers. Their issuance is therefore based on a different strategy.

It was also noted (by Canada) that in the past two years, there has been slightly wider bid-offer spreads in government bonds due to increased regulation on the balance sheet of dealers, among other things. It was also noted (by Germany) that new regulatory requirements for liquidity have resulted in larger government bond (Bund) positions.

Table 3.4. **How does the liquidity of sovereign bonds compare to non-sovereign bonds issued in the domestic market?**

Country-by country overview	
Australia	The Australian Government Securities market is significantly more liquid than every other Australian dollar fixed income market.
Austria	Sovereign are 100% liquid. Relatively liquidity versus other bond classes is 20% (Government Agencies) and 5% (Corporates, including Banks).
Belgium	Other issuers in our domestic market are much smaller and cannot provide the same liquidity. Their issuance is based on a different strategy.
Canada	The bid-offer on domestic Government of Canada bonds tends to be at least half as wide as many other Canadian issuer classes (i.e. Provincial bonds, Canada Mortgage Bonds, corporate bonds). In the past 2 years, there has been slightly wider bid-offer spreads in bonds due to increased regulation on the balance sheet of dealers, among other things. Canada's experience is in line with that of most other countries in the world.
Chile	Even in markets where Treasury bonds are not highly liquid, demand is strong. This enables the construction of the local currency yield curve which market players use as pricing reference. However, corporate issuers are normally smaller issuers and corporate bonds are much less liquidity. Moreover, even local companies with higher financing needs that are issuing in larger sizes often decide *not* to access the domestic market but, instead, to tap external markets.
Czech Republic	Domestic sovereign bonds (MoF) are highly liquid in comparison to corporate bonds.
Denmark	The Danish market for mortgage bonds is quite large (the outstanding volume is more than 100 per cent of Danish GDP) but the number of outstanding mortgage bonds is also large and hence the volume in some of the series might be quite modest. On the other hand, ongoing issuances in the mortgage bond series support liquidity. Studies show that the liquidity of Danish mortgage bonds is quite similar to Danish government bonds (see note 1).
Finland	No estimates are available.
France	French government bonds are the most liquid securities in the French domestic market.
Germany	Exact figures are not available. However, German government bonds (Bunds) are far more liquid than corporate bonds. Any desired volume is executable in any market situation. Bunds have proven to be the most liquid assets especially in times of uncertainty. New regulatory requirements for liquidity have resulted in larger Bund positions. Bunds are the underlying securities for Eurex future contracts – the most liquid contracts in the world.
Hungary	Accurate data are not available. However, secondary market trading and turnover of other (non-sovereign) bonds are relatively negligible. Government bonds and Treasury bills are the most liquid products of the Hungarian securities market; they account for close to 100% of the total secondary market trading.
Iceland	The turnover of bonds (a measure of liquidity) in the different classes during the last 6 months is as follows: Treasury bonds account for 87% of total turnover, the Housing Financing Fund (HFF; which is a government agency) 10%, municipalities 1%, corporates 1%, and financials 1%.
Ireland	Irish government bonds have been quite liquid over the last year, with spreads normalising. However, liquidity and turnover are somewhat reduced over the last few months following QE and general Euro Area liquidity tightening.
Israel	Generally, sovereign bonds are far more liquid than other issuers in the domestic market. The average daily trading volume in government bonds on the Tel-Aviv Stock Exchange (TASE) in 2014 was ILS 3 225 Million, while the daily turnover in the corporate bonds market was ILS 1 020 Million.
Italy	The Italian bond market has relatively few large issuers. Government bonds are far more liquid than large corporate bonds including financials. Bid-ask spreads on the secondary market of government bonds are normally three to four times narrower than spreads on larger corporate bonds.
Japan	Based on the turnover ratio, JGBs have a higher liquidity than the bonds issued by other classes of issuers. For instance, let the turnover ratio of JGBs be 100%, then that ratio of other local currency bonds is about 36% in May 2015 (note: the JGB share in the total outstanding amount of Yen Bonds is about 80%).
Korea	On the basis of average daily trading volumes, the liquidity of sovereign bonds is USD 11.9 billion (KRW 13.4 trillion), and that of other bonds is USD 4.6 billion (KRW 5.2 trillion).
Luxembourg	Information is not available.
Mexico	The government securities are much more liquid than the rest of the fixed-income securities traded in the Mexican market. For example, in 2015, corporate securities traded between banks have a daily average of MXN 3.6 billion (approximately USD 229 million), while interbank operations involving government securities have a daily average of MXN 21 billion (USD 1.3 billion). It is worth noting that as of February 2015, Mexican corporate debt securities (called Cebures) are serviced by Euroclear (prior to this date, only government securities were included in this platform). This feature will be instrumental to provide more liquidity to Cebures.
Netherlands	Information is not available.
New Zealand	Domestic sovereign bonds are more liquid than other issuers in the domestic market, having the largest bond programme, the largest amount on issue and the lowest borrowing costs of NZD issuers. The NZD Government bond programme serves as an important benchmark for other domestic issuers across the curve.
Poland	Non-sovereign domestic bonds (corporates, municipalities and other issuers) have relatively poor liquidity. Their liquidity ratio (based on data from WSE Bond Market – Catalyst) has not exceeded 0.3% in recent months.

Table 3.4. **How does the liquidity of sovereign bonds compare to non-sovereign bonds issued in the domestic market?** *(cont.)*

Country-by country overview	
Portugal	Although data on the liquidity of non-sovereign securities is not available, one would expect it to be lower than the liquidity of sovereign bonds.
Slovak Republic	Assuming that sovereign bonds are 100% liquid, then, by way of comparison, non-sovereign bonds are only 5% liquid.
Slovenia	As the end of June 2015, total capitalisation of bonds on the Ljubljana Stock Exchange amounted to 23.1 bn EUR; of which 74.6% of this capitalisation refers to domestic government bonds and the rest to bonds issued by banks, corporations and insurance companies. These figures give a rough indication of potential liquidity for each class of issuer. Out of 19 outstanding domestic currency government bond lines, 17 were issued via the local CSD (i.e. the Central Securities Clearing Corporation Ljubljana or KDD). Accordingly, based on data from the KDD register at the end of 2012, 2013, 2014 and 30 June 2015, the total nominal value of domestic currency government securities issued via the KDD was EUR 14.3 bn, EUR 12.4 bn, EUR 14.0 bn and EUR 13.9 bn, respectively. These figures represent 91.7%, 75.3%, 81.7% and 82.0% of the total nominal value of all debt securities issued via the KDD.
Spain	The liquidity of sovereign bonds is much higher than the liquidity of bonds issued by sub-sovereign authorities. It is also much higher than the liquidity of bonds issued by other official institutions (like ICO) or agencies (like FADE).
Switzerland	On the domestic side, the Swiss Government, together with two Swiss mortgage institutions (Pfandbriefbank and Pfandbriefzentrale), are the most important domestic issuers. Confederation bonds currently account for 25% of outstanding domestic bonds whereas the two Pfandbriefe institutions together have a market share of almost 30%. The bonds issued by the Swiss Government and the two mortgage institutions are the most liquid segments. In fact, Swiss bond traders judge mortgage bonds as more liquid than Confederation bonds. However, measured in terms of trading volumes, Confederation bonds are by far the most important bond category, accounting for around half of all transaction volumes in the domestic segment of the market. On average, S Fr. 3.5 billion of Confederation bonds are traded every month. In 2014, the total trading volume in Confederation bonds amounted to around 40 billion (i.e. around half of outstanding bonds changed hands). But in terms of the number of trades, the share of Confederation bonds is only between 10-20%.
Turkey	Although the amount of non-sovereign bond issuances has increased since 2010, secondary market liquidity mostly consists of sovereign bonds.
United Kingdom	UK Government bonds are much more liquid than other issuers in GBP, given the differences in the scale of issuance and sizes of outstanding bonds, although frequent borrowers (e.g. EIB and KfW) have established sterling curves, with benchmark issues that exceed USD 1bn in size.

Note: For more information see Buchholst, Birgitte Vølund: Liquidity in Danish Covered and Government Bonds, Danmarks Nationalbank, *Monetary Review* 1, Quarter 2011, Part 1.
Source: Responses to the 2015 survey on liquidity in secondary markets for governments bonds by the OECD Working Party on Debt Management.

3.6. Liquidity in bond derivatives markets in the OECD area

This section provides a liquidity assessment of bond derivatives in comparison to the liquidity of (underlying) government cash (physical) bonds in OECD countries. Table 3.5 provides a general summary of the responses, while Table 3.6 provides details on the situation in the different OECD markets.

Table 3.5. **Summary of survey findings on the liquidity of bond derivatives in comparison to cash bonds**

	Percentage of answers*			
	Yes		No	
Q1.: Do you have a liquid bond derivatives market?	50%		50%	
	Better	Equal	Worse	Liquidity varies across maturities or is difficult to measure
Q2. If yes, how does liquidity in that market compare to liquidity of the underlying cash bonds?	10.0%	3.3%	20.0%	16.7%

* All percentages are calculated on the basis of the total number of answers (30).
Source: Responses to the 2015 survey on liquidity in secondary markets for governments bonds by the OECD Working Party on Debt Management.

Table 3.6. Country-by-country overview of liquidity of bond derivatives in comparison to cash bonds

	Do you have a liquid bond derivatives market?		How does liquidity in that market compare to liquidity of the underlying cash bonds?
	Yes	No	
Australia	x		Better
Austria		x	
Belgium		x	
Canada	x		Liquidity varies across maturities
Chile	x		Liquidity varies across maturities
Czech Republic		x	
Denmark		x	
Finland		x	
France	x		Lower
Germany	x		Better
Hungary		x	
Iceland		x	
Ireland		x	
Israel	x		Lower
Italy	x		Difficult to measure
Japan	x		Difficult to measure
Korea	x		Equal
Luxembourg		x	
Mexico	x		Lower
Netherlands		x	
New Zealand		x	
Norway		x	
Poland	x		Lower
Portugal		x	
Slovak Republic	x		Lower
Slovenia		x	
Spain	x		Lower
Switzerland	x		Better
Turkey		x	
United Kingdom	x		Liquidity varies across maturities
Total	15	15	

Table 3.6. Liquidity of bond derivatives in comparison to cash bonds (continuation with country notes)

Austria	There is no derivative market for government bonds (RAGB). Hedging is usually done via the highly liquid German Bund Futures market.
Belgium	Since the introduction of the euro, a futures market for Belgian government bonds does not exist any longer. Investors and traders are using the German and French futures markets.
Canada	Liquidity varies across term types. Derivatives (bond futures) are more liquid than physical bonds in the 10-year sector, where liquidity is the highest. Liquidity in the futures market for 5 years and 2 years is good, although trading volumes are lower than that for the 10 years. The 30-year sector has only one type of derivatives, the 30-year Government of Canada bond futures (LGB).
Chile	Liquidity varies across term types. Liquidity in derivative market is equal for cash bonds up to 10 years and lower for cash bonds with a higher maturity.
Czech Republic	The Czech Republic does not have a (liquid) bond derivatives market.
Denmark	There is no market for futures on Danish government bonds.
Finland	Finland does not have a bond derivatives market.
France	Future contracts exist for 10-year and 5-year nominal French government bonds (Eurex). There is also a sovereign CDS market for French debt. The liquidity on these instruments is lower than that of the cash market.
Hungary	Hungary does not have a (liquid) bond derivatives market.
Iceland	There is no active domestic bond derivatives market in Iceland.

Table 3.6. **Liquidity of bond derivatives in comparison to cash bonds (continuation with country notes)**

Ireland	Although Ireland has no domestic liquid bond derivatives markets, being a member of the Eurozone provides market participants with other options. Investors and traders can use the derivatives of other Euro markets for hedging purposes (for example, the German and French futures markets).
Italy	Liquidity in the Italian BTP futures market has improved since the 2013 Survey, as evidenced by an increase in "open interest" and "the average volume of contracts". The level of liquidity in the futures market begins to approach that of the cash market, although it is difficult to make an accurate comparison (given the structural differences between the two markets).
Japan	Japan has derivatives markets for JGB futures, JGB futures options and JGB spot options. However, it is difficult to assess their relative liquidity on the basis of an accurate comparison because liquidity of each product is being influenced largely by (changing) market circumstance.
Luxembourg	Luxembourg does not have a bond derivatives market.
Mexico	The spot market is much more liquid than the bond derivatives market. MexDer, the Mexican Derivatives Exchange, is still a developing market. As of today, there are futures contracts for the 3-, 5-, 10-, 20- and 30-year MBonds benchmarks. Up to March 2014, the most used futures contract was the 10-year MBond with an annual average volume of 1.5 trillion contracts. (Each futures contract on the Mexican Derivatives Exchange covers a total of 1 000 MBonds, equivalent to a face value of MXN 100 000.) However, these contracts have a package of deliverable bonds but since these bonds are not equally liquid, MexDer decided to list futures contracts for the most liquid MBonds on the spot market (i.e. those with maturities on Dec-2024 and May-2031). Since 2014, 64% of the volume of Mbonds future contracts corresponds to the Dec-2024 and May-2031 contracts. This measure also contributed to increase the number of participants in this market. Prior to the introduction of these contracts there were only 6 active counterparts. After the introduction of the new futures contracts, this number increased to 17 active participants. It is also worth noting that financial institutions have more incentives to trade these securities since they are granted extra points to their Market Makers rankings for every bid/ask quote. With a wider investors base, the bid/ask spread for the MBonds futures contracts can be expected to decrease while the "open interest" for these contracts increases. The investors' base can further widen, considering that only 50% of the Pension Funds are currently certified to invest in this kind of securities and the rest are in the process of obtaining that certification. Although MexDer has implemented modifications to adapt its working procedures to comply with international regulations, it will have to offer more incentives for investors to participate in this derivatives exchange.
Netherlands	No information is available.
New Zealand	New Zealand does not have a direct bond derivative market. Participants typically use either NZD Interest Rate Swaps or AUD Bond futures to cover positions should it be necessary. Although these are not a perfect hedge, both derivatives products would have more liquidity than the physical bond market.
Norway	Norway does not have a bond derivatives market.
Poland	Treasury bond futures contracts are traded on the WSE (the Warsaw Stock Exchange). The underlying instruments are fixed rate and zero-coupon Treasury bonds issued by the Minister of Finance with an issue value not less than PLN 2.5 billion. Liquidity of the market is very poor (26 transactions with a total turnover of USD 13 million in the first half of 2015).
Portugal	Portugal does not have a bond derivatives market.
Slovak Republic	The Slovak Republic has only a very limited derivative market (ASW on demand). Liquidity in this derivatives market is lower than in the physical bond market.
Slovenia	The Slovenian domestic currency government bonds are denominated in Euros and therefore investors and traders can use the liquid derivatives of other Euro markets for hedging purposes.
Switzerland	Switzerland has a bond future market (CONF Futures), which is not very liquid compared to the Euro Bund Futures. The deliverable products for the CONF Futures contract (6% coupon) are Swiss debt securities with remaining maturity of 8 to 13 years. It is assumed that the CONF Futures market is more liquid than the Federal bonds market.
Turkey	Turkey does not have a bond derivatives market.
United Kingdom	The ICE Futures Europe lists four UK Government bond futures contracts, with notional maturities of 2-, 5-, 10- and 30-years. Liquidity is better for the 10-year futures contract and lower for the 2-, 5- and 30-year contracts. GBP interest rate and inflation swaps are also widely quoted and actively traded.

Note:

1. 30 countries answered these questions.
2. Austria, Belgium, Czech Republic, Finland, Hungary, Iceland, Ireland, Luxembourg, Netherlands, Norway, Portugal and Turkey do not have a derivatives market or information is not available.

Source: Responses to the 2015 survey on liquidity in secondary markets for governments bonds by the OECD Working Party on Debt Management.

The market structure for derivatives differs considerably. Table 3.5 shows that 15 OECD countries (50% of responses) have a liquid bond derivatives market. However, the assessment of the relative liquidity of that market (in comparison to the underlying market for government cash bonds) differs considerable across countries. It was noted that the measurement of liquidity may be difficult or complicated by the fact that liquidity varies across maturities or term types (see Table 3.6 for a summary of the responses per country). For example, derivatives (bond futures) in Canada are more liquid than physical bonds in the 10-year sector, where liquidity is the highest. Liquidity in the futures market for 5 years and 2 years is good, although trading volumes are lower than that for the 10 years. The 30-year sector has only one type of derivatives, the 30-year Government of Canada bond futures (LGB).

The situation in the Eurozone has special characteristics. Although several Euro countries have no domestic liquid bond derivatives markets, being a member of the Eurozone provides market participants with other (or additional) options. Investors and traders from jurisdictions without a (liquid) derivatives market can use the (liquid) derivatives of other Euro markets for hedging purposes.

Liquidity in several futures markets has improved since the last couple of years, as evidenced by an increase in "open interest" and "the average volume of contracts" (for example, the Italian BTP futures and the Mexican MBonds futures).

3.7. Liquidity of the repo market for government bonds

A highly liquid repo market for government bonds is an important component of the market infrastructure for trading government bonds. The repo rate functions often as an important market signal. Against this backdrop, DMOs were asked to give an evaluation of the degree of liquidity of the repo market for their sovereign bonds (using a score from 5 [highly liquid] to 1[illiquid]).

A total of twenty-five (25) DMOs returned a liquidity score for their repo market in government bonds. Figure 3.4 shows that 10 DMOs (i.e. 40% of responses) judge their repo market for government bonds as highly liquid (i.e. score 5), while only two out of 25 responses (or 8%) consider their repo market as illiquid (see Table 3.7 for more details, including country specific notes).

Figure 3.4. **How liquid is the repo market for government bonds?**

Percentages*

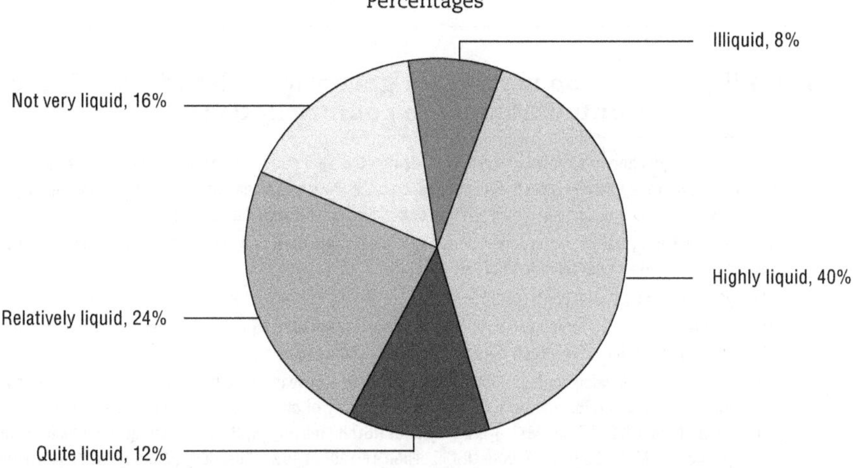

* All percentages are calculated on the basis of 25 (out of 30) responses.

Source: Responses to the 2015 survey on liquidity in secondary markets for governments bonds by the OECD Working Party on Debt Management.

StatLink http://dx.doi.org/10.1787/888933393213

Several countries observed that liquidity is good in the repo market, although some tightness is evident in the repo market. The combined effects of lower interest rate and more regulatory pressure on dealers' balance sheets are judged as having played role in (regular) repo tightness in some government bond lines (with no concentration in particular sectors; see, for example, Canada; Table 3.7).

Table 3.7. **Liquidity of the repo market for government bonds in OECD countries**

	Highly liquid (= 5)	Quite liquid (= 4)	Relatively liquid (= 3)	Not very liquid (= 2)	illiquid (= 1)
Australia	x				
Austria	x				
Belgium	x				
Canada			x		
Chile				x	
Czech Republic			x		
Denmark		x			
Finland			x		
France	x				
Germany	x				
Hungary			x		
Ireland	x				
Israel					x
Italy	x				
Korea			x		
Luxembourg					
Mexico	x				
Netherlands	x				
New Zealand	x				
Norway				x	
Poland		x			
Portugal				x	
Slovak Republic				x	
Slovenia					x
Spain		x			
Switzerland			x		
Total	10	3	6	4	2

Table 3.7. **Liquidity of the repo market for government bonds in OECD countries (continuation with country notes)**

Canada	Liquidity is good, although some tightness is evident in the repo market. Combining the effects of lower interest rate in Canada and more regulatory pressure on dealers' balance sheets, Canada has observed regular repo tightness in selective Government of Canada bonds with no concentration in particular sectors.
Denmark	The repo market for Danish government bonds is relatively liquid. Repos are often executed because of bond traders' demand for the underlying bond in the repo.
Iceland	There is no active domestic bond repo market.
Japan	Japan has markets for SC repo and GC repo. Assessing the degree of liquidity is judged as difficult, because the liquidity of each product is influenced largely by specific market circumstances.
Mexico	The repo markets in Mexico are highly developed and liquid. Key features of these markets are: i) both repo transactions involving government bonds and bank bonds have a maturity of only one day; ii) the daily average volume for government bonds in 2015 was MXN 1 trillion (about USD 80 billion); iii) the daily average volume for bank bonds in the same period was MXN 125 billion (about USD 9 billion); iv) about 40% of the daily volume is traded through an electronic platform, and the rest is done by phone; and v) market participants include banks, pension funds, private investors, public entities and corporates.
Netherlands	The Dutch DMO offers PDs an emergency back-up facility which costs -25 Bps for regular market trades. This facility provides PDs the possibility to cover their shorts. During the last few months, a significant increase in the use of this facility has been observed.

Table 3.7. **Liquidity of the repo market for government bonds in OECD countries (continuation with country notes)**

New Zealand	Repo market is very liquid but characterised as being short-term in nature (out to one week). The Repo market is used for both bond management activities (covering short positions in the market) as well as cash management purposes. Both activities provide natural interest for the development of the short-term market – however activity is concentrated to nominal bonds with IIB being less activity traded. Longer-term repo does occur from time to time but this appears to be direct contact between investors and intermediaries.
Poland	The repo market for domestic bonds is fairly liquid. The liquidity ratio for repo transactions exceeds the one for outright trades. Repo transactions constitute about 75% of the secondary market.
Portugal	Some bonds are difficult to find in the market (because of their reduced outstanding stock and/or high level of concentration in "buy and hold" portfolios). As a result, also the repo market is affected.
Slovak Republic	The PDs judge the repo market as "not very liquid but improving".
Switzerland	It is judged that the liquidity of the repo market for Swiss Federal bonds is moderate due to the fact that many securities are bought and hold until maturity by institutional investors. Nevertheless, since 2011, the share of repo transactions, collateralised with bonds issued by the Swiss Confederation, has increased significantly (from 0.10% to 0.70% market share). One reason could be the negative yield situation in the Swiss franc zone which has put collateral used in the repo market in the spotlight (and not cash).
United Kingdom	Liquidity is concentrated around overnight repo, which is highly liquid and decreases with maturity. Repos with maturities > 1 month are generally illiquid. Anecdotal evidence suggests that liquidity has deteriorated slightly in recent years.

Source: Responses to the 2015 survey on liquidity in secondary markets for governments bonds by OECD Working Party on Debt Management.

Other DMOs report that liquidity in repo markets is affected by the concentration of bonds in buy and hold portfolios (see, for example, Table 3.7: Portugal and Switzerland).

Repo markets are usually short-term in nature (sometimes a maturity of just 1 day like in the case of Mexico or out to one week in the case of New Zealand; see Table 7). The repo market is used for bond management activities (covering short positions in the market) and/or for cash management purposes. As noted by the New Zealand DMO, both activities provide a natural interest for the development of the short end of the market.

3.8. Transparency of bond markets and related information flows

This section discusses the responses by OECD DMOs regarding the evaluation (scoring) of the transparency in their government bond market and related information flows.

Twenty-nine (29 out of 30) DMOs returned a transparency score for their government bond market and related information flows (see Figure 3.5).

Figure 3.5. **Transparency of bond markets and related information flows**

Percentages*

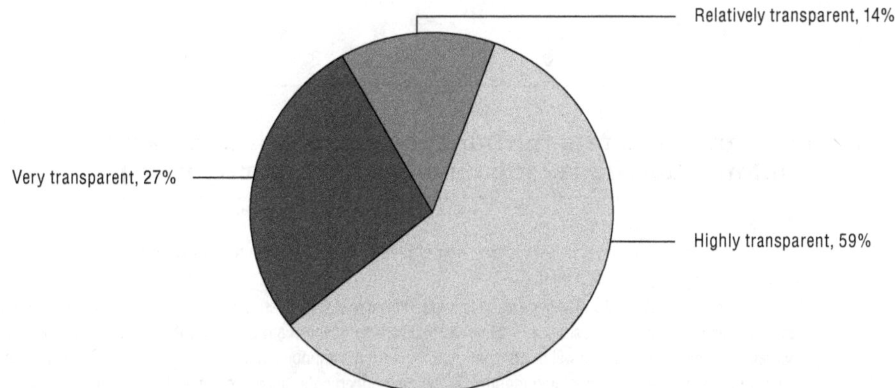

* All percentages are calculated on the basis of 29 out of 30 responses.

Source: Responses to the 2015 survey on liquidity in secondary markets for governments bonds by the OECD Working Party on Debt Management.

StatLink http://dx.doi.org/10.1787/888933393227

A majority of 17 DMOs (59%) judge their market and related information flows as highly transparent (which is equal to the maximum score of 5 while a score of 1 denotes a non-transparent situation). Eight DMOs (27% of the responding DMOs) consider their bond market and information flow as very transparent. Only 14% of the countries perceive their bond market as "relatively transparent" (see Table 3.8 for more detailed responses including some country specific notes).

Table 3.8. **How would you rate the transparency of bond markets and related information flows?**

	Highly transparent (= 5)	Very transparent (= 4)	Relatively transparent (= 3)	Not very transparent (= 2)	Non-transparent (= 1)
Australia	x				
Austria	x				
Belgium	x				
Canada		x			
Chile			x		
Czech Republic	x				
Denmark	x				
Finland		x			
France		x			
Germany	x				
Hungary		x			
Iceland	x				
Ireland	x				
Israel	x				
Italy	x				
Japan	x				
Korea	x				
Luxembourg	x				
Mexico	x				
Netherlands	x				
New Zealand		x			
Norway			x		
Poland	x				
Portugal			x		
Slovenia			x		
Spain		x			
Switzerland		x			
Turkey		x			
United Kingdom	x				
Total	17	8	4	0	0

Table 3.8. **How would you rate the transparency of bond markets and related information flows? (*continuation with country notes*)**

Canada	Information flows are transparent.
Chile	Pension funds, the main player in the system, are required by law to execute their operations through a stock exchange, which make them highly transparent.
Denmark	Twice a year, the Danish DMO releases key information about the public debt strategy. In December, the announcement describes the target for i) the issuance of domestic and foreign government bonds for the following year and ii) the bond segments in which the issuance will be concentrated. In June, the announcement follows up on the first part of the year and outlines the strategy for the remaining months. These announcements (and much other information) are released via our website. These information releases regarding the Danish government bond market contribute to a high degree of transparency. Danish government bonds are primarily sold via regular auctions supplemented with tap sales. The auctions are conducted through the MTS Denmark auction system with the primary dealers as counterparties. The auction procedure

Table 3.8. **How would you rate the transparency of bond markets and related information flows? *(continuation with country notes)***

	can be summarised in four steps: 1) Announcement of auction calendar, 2) Choice of government securities for auction, 3) Pricing, bids and allotment, and 4) Announcement of auction results. Primary dealers are committed to quote current bid-ask prices on one or more platforms (within the framework agreed upon in co-operation between DMO and the primary dealer group). Ongoing price quotation on electronic trading platforms enables market participants to monitor market developments and conduct transactions at prices and volumes known in advance. This *pre-trade* information fosters transparency and supports efficient price formation in the market for government securities.
France	Information flows in French bond market are very transparent.
Japan	Information on JGBs is made public via the Osaka exchange, Japan Bond Trading, the Japan Securities Dealers Association, etc.
Mexico	Transparency and information flows in the Mexican bond market meet the high standards of market participants.
Netherlands	The Dutch DMO announces the issuing calendar for government securities at the beginning of the year. This updated every quarter. All upcoming issues are communicated to the market one week before via Bloomberg, the website of the DMO as well as Twitter. All issuance details, such as outstanding volumes, are made public via the website.
New Zealand	Given the changes to the way investors now interact with intermediaries, information directly related to client flows are perhaps now not as directly advertised to the market than in the past and may take longer to filter through the market. Other market information flows are highly transparent. There is the potential for rate transparency to be undermined during periods of global market volatility as investors step away from the market. The resulting lack of flow means that price transparency during these periods may be undermined. This is particularly true for any bond that has not traded during the day given market participants sensitivities around providing benchmark (closing) prices. This has on occasion caused issues in the primary market as indicative market pricing has not been supportive of a bid from institutional investors.
Portugal	Market is relatively transparent. However, since the turnover is mostly OTC, transparency is limited. Since the implementation of the new HRF reporting format (Harmonized Reporting Format), liquidity has been increased.
Slovak Republic	The opinions of Primary Dealers (PDs) vary from non-transparent (mainly foreign PDs) to very transparent (domestic PDs). Transparency is higher in the primary market because a devoted electronic platform for secondary market transactions is absent.
Turkey	On the last business day of October, the "Annual Treasury Financing Programme" is published on the web page of the Turkish Treasury. This annual report announces the total amount that the Turkish government is planning to borrow in both domestic and external markets. In addition, the Treasury announces every month the borrowing plan for the next 3 months, including auction dates and details about the securities to be issued. Moreover, the exchange (Borsa Istanbul) publishes daily details about secondary market transactions, including average interest rate, total volume of transactions, etc.
United Kingdom	The DMO treats all Primary Dealers (PDs) as equals in its dealings, wherever possible ensuring that all are privy to the same levels of information when conducting any market-sensitive activities. Before the beginning of each financial year the DMO pre-announces the details of its issuance plans to the market, including an auction calendar setting out the dates and gilt types for the year ahead, and details on planned average auction sizes. Details on the maturities of the gilts to be issued are pre-announced in advance of each quarter. The DMO also provides via its website (www.dmo.gov.uk) a whole host of data and information on all aspects of the gilt-edged market. Moreover, PD sales desks reportedly cover all relevant information flows to investors, including auction and syndication announcements and other press releases by the DMO.

Source: Responses to the 2015 survey on liquidity in secondary markets for governments bonds by OECD Working Party on Debt Management.

3.9. Liquidity and the performance of the infrastructure of government bond markets

Table 3.9 shows that according to 80% of responding OECD DMOs, the current infrastructure performs well, without an adverse impact on liquidity in the government bond market. In most of these jurisdictions the existing infrastructure works smoothly and therefore (as of 30 June 2015) no changes are required to enhance market liquidity.

The rest of the responding DMOs (20%) noted several issues related to the market infrastructure, sometimes with a link to liquidity. For example, the New Zealand DMO received feedback that the lack of a NZD futures market reduces liquidity in the physical (cash) market (see Table 3.10 for some country specific notes).

Other DMOs report that they have implemented, or are planning to introduce, improvements in the market infrastructure. For example, recently significant improvements were made in the Japanese market infrastructure, including i) resumption of ultra-long (20-year) JGB futures trading and extension of the trading time for futures at the Osaka Exchange;

Table 3.9. Summary of answers on liquidity and government bond market infrastructure

	Percentage of answers*	
	No, current market infrastructure performs well	Yes, changes in market infrastructure maybe desirable
Are there performance issues with the market infrastructure (e.g. settlement and clearing systems, flash trading, etc.) of which some of them may be linked to liquidity problems in your bond market?	80% (24 countries)	20% (6 countries)

* All percentages are calculated on the basis of 30 responses.

Source: Responses to the 2015 survey on liquidity in secondary markets for governments bonds by the OECD Working Party on Debt Management.

Table 3.10. Infrastructure aspects that have an impact on bond market liquidity

	Country-by country overview
Hungary	The current infrastructure works smoothly.
Israel	Trading on the Tel Aviv Stock Exchange takes place between Sunday and Thursday. In order to encourage foreign investment in Israel's capital market, the Tel Aviv Stock Exchange (TASE) is currently examining the possibility of aligning its trading schedule with the accepted practice from abroad by adopting a Monday through Friday trading week.
Italy	*Express II* is a highly performing settlement and central depository system managed by Monte Titoli, the Italian Central Securities Depository. Monte Titoli will join Target-2 Securities (T2S), managed by the Eurosystem, later this year. Flash traders (understood here as high frequency-trading or *Algo* trading) are fairly active on the BTP futures market. However, this type of trading activities is not relevant for the cash market.
Japan	According to "the Japan Securities Dealers Association", a shortening of settlement periods to "T+1" for outright trading is being planned for the first half of 2018. Moreover, the "Advisory Council for Government Debt Management" noted in recent reports (made public on June 18, 2014 and June 16, 2015) that recently there has been significant progress in the market infrastructure, including i) resumption of ultra-long (20-year) JGB futures trading and extension of the trading time for futures at the Osaka Exchange; ii) Better access to trading JGBs from abroad by extending the operation hours of the government bond settlement system operated by the BoJ.
Mexico	The settlement and clearing systems used in the Mexican market operate adequately.
Netherlands	The current infrastructure works well.
New Zealand	Anecdotally the NZDMO receives feedback that the lack of a NZD futures market reduces liquidity in the physical market.
Poland	There are no significant issues regarding the infrastructure that have an impact on the liquidity in the Polish bond market.
Slovak Republic	Settlement system without bridge to pan-European settlement systems like Euroclear bridge to Clearstream and very high fees for settlement for domestic banks.
Slovenia	The local CSD (KDD) has a semi-direct link established with the ICSD's (Euroclear and Clearstream banking). This allows investors to hold government bonds in the securities accounts of either KDD, Euroclear or Clearstream. This is a relevant feature for almost all of the domestic currency bonds (currently 17 out of the 19 outstanding domestic currency bond lines are issued using the local CSD).
Spain	At some points during the European sovereign debt crisis, Spain experienced the systemic influence that CCPs (central counterparties) may exert. Large haircuts, imposed by international CCPs in response to lower ratings and higher volatility (during these crisis episodes), created major challenges for domestic investors in carrying out repo operations through these CCPs.

Source: Responses to the 2015 survey on liquidity in secondary markets for governments bonds by OECD Working Party on Debt Management.

ii) Better access to trading JGBs from abroad by extending the operation hours of the government bond settlement system operated by the BoJ. In addition, a shortening of settlement periods to "T+1" for outright trading is being planned for the first half of 2018.

Crisis episodes may sometimes influence the smooth functioning of the market infrastructure. For example, the Spanish DMO observed that large haircuts, imposed by international CCPs in response to lower ratings and higher volatility (during the European sovereign debt crisis), created major challenges for domestic investors in carrying out repo operations through these CCPs.

3.10. Indicators of liquidity problems in government bond markets

In this part of the survey, DMOs gave information about the most prominent indicators they use when there are liquidity problems in their government bond markets. For example, size of bid-ask spreads, increased volatility, lower turnover, reduction of trade sizes, failed trades, a narrowing investor base, and higher yields.

Twenty-two OECD DMOs (out of 30) answered questions related to this issue. The responses in Table 3.11 indicate that there are some indicators that DMOs commonly use when there are liquidity problems such as wide bid-offer spreads (64%), decrease of trade size (32%) and a narrowing investor base (32%). Higher yields and increased volatility score a bit lower (23%).

Table 3.11. Overview of indicators for liquidity problems

	Percentage of answers*						
	Size of bid-ask spreads (e.g. wide bid-offer spreads)	Increased volatility	Lower turnover	Decrease in trade sizes	Failed trades	Narrowing investor base	Higher yields
If liquidity were a problem in your bond market, what would be the most prominent indicators of this?	64	23	14	32	14	32	23

Table 3.11. Overview of indicators for liquidity problems (continuation with country notes)

Australia	If liquidity were a problem it would be manifested in "wide bid-offer spreads", 'increased volatility' and "falling turnover".
Austria	One would observe "lower trade volumes" on the screens of market makers, with "widening bid/offer spreads".
Canada	The prominent indicators of problematic liquidity include the number and volume of securities lending operations from the Bank of Canada, the "size of bid-ask spreads", and "the degree to which trade sizes have decreased".
Chile	Although there are no formal measures of the degree of participation of foreign investors in the government bond markets available, informal assessments found this to be a negligible factor for explaining liquidity problems. Moreover, a large part of the outstanding stock of domestic government securities is being held by the domestic pension funds, which behave as "buy-and-hold" investors.
Denmark	The yields on Danish government bonds usually are close to the yields on German government bonds. Hence, "changes in the spread to German bunds" can be an indicator of liquidity problems. In addition, poor liquidity can be signalled by other factors such as "low trade volumes", "higher bid-ask spreads" (reported by primary dealers) or "larger observed price movements during transactions".
Finland	Some investors that claim that the market is less liquid (or even illiquid), often do not participate.
Hungary	Generally, liquidity always could be improved. Liquidity problems can sometimes be observed in certain market situations due to the lack of a diversified local institutional investor base (local banks are the most important investors). In temporary situations with liquidity problems one can observe that spreads widen and, interestingly, the share and use of the electronic trading platform (MTS Hungary) increases vis-a-vis the OTC market.
Ireland	"Higher bid-offer spreads" and "low(er) turnover" are important indicators.
Israel	Only some inflation-indexed bonds have liquidity problems.
Italy	Liquidity problems are detected mainly through distortions in the interpolated yield curve, pronounced specialness in the repo market, and failed trades. Naturally, these events may be interconnected.
Japan	The Japanese DMO monitors the following indicators: "bid-ask spread", "best bid-ask sizes", "trading volumes", "historical price volatility" and "the turnover ratio".
Luxembourg	One would observe "higher yields" and "investors avoiding the market".
Mexico	One would observe a "widening of bid/ask spreads" and "higher yields".
Netherlands	One would observe "lower trading volumes", "higher bid-ask spreads" and signals/information provided by PDs.
New Zealand	When liquidity appears to become a problem: 1) Global bond market volatility heightened; 2) General consensus themes being undertaken by investors (either bid or offer) than concentrate risk with intermediaries; 3) Daily traded volume falls.
Norway	One would observe higher yields and investors avoiding the market.

Table 3.11. **Overview of indicators for liquidity problems (*continuation with country notes*)**

Poland	In normal times, indicators like "failed trades" or "certain investors are avoiding the market" do not signal the presence of structural liquidity problems in the Polish government bond market. Although temporal distortions in global markets can affect the functioning of the domestic market (e.g. in the form of higher spreads), this does not imply that the domestic bond market inherently suffers from liquidity problems.
Portugal	Some (categories of) investors are still avoiding the Portuguese bond market, especially in periods with high(er) volatility.
Slovak Republic	The government bond market is fairly illiquid due to the following reasons. i) The main factor is the relatively small outstanding amount of debt. ii) Moreover, most of the bonds are in portfolios that are being held until maturity (banking books, pension funds, insurers etc.) Hence, a very small part is available for trading, including market making. iii) Regulations also play a role. iv) An electronic platform for concentrating liquidity is absent. v) A non-functioning repo market has also an adverse impact on market liquidity. vi) ECB's QE programme drains liquidity from the market. Against this backdrop, PDs report "failed trades", "that certain investors are avoiding the market" and "wider bid offer spreads".
Slovenia	Indicators for liquidity problems include "a lower volume of trade", "wider bid/ask spreads" and spreads over mid-swaps", and "smaller trade sizes".
Spain	The range of indicators signalling these temporary problems has been quite diverse: "widening bid-ask spreads", "higher yields" and to some extent "failed trades". "Volatility" as an indicator of liquidity problems is ambiguous.
Switzerland	Indicators for liquidity problems include "higher spreads between bid and ask".
Turkey	Most of the transactions in the secondary market involve foreign investors. Hence, when foreign investors are not active in the secondary market, total transaction volumes decrease significantly, resulting in declining market liquidity. Moreover, in recent years, the share of bonds held by public funds is rising. Since these investors are of the buy-and-hold type, secondary market liquidity is affected to some degree.
United Kingdom	Occasional "wider bid-offer spreads" and "price-gapping" are indicative of a less liquid gilt market. This usually occurs in periods of "heightened market volatility", when investors typically "decrease their participation" in the gilt market.

* All percentages are calculated on the basis of 22 responses out of 30.
Source: Responses to the 2015 survey on liquidity in secondary markets for governments bonds by the OECD Working Party on Debt Management.

Other indicators, mentioned by some DMOs, include: distortions on interpolated yield curve (e.g. Italy), and an increase in the share of electronic platform transactions compared to OTC (e.g. Hungary). Also "price-gapping" can be indicative of a less liquid market. This usually occurs in periods of "heightened market volatility", when investors typically "decrease their participation" in the gilt market (see, for example, the UK in Table 3.11).

Smaller markets, such as the Slovak Republic (Table 3.11), argue that their market is fairly illiquid due to the following reasons. i) An important structural reason is the relatively small outstanding amount of debt. ii) Moreover, most of the bonds are in portfolios that are being held until maturity, which means that a very small part is available for trading, including market making. iii) Sometimes an electronic platform for concentrating liquidity is absent; while also a non-functioning repo market might have an adverse impact on market liquidity. It was also noted by the Slovak Republic that ECB's QE programme is draining liquidity from the market.

3.11. Which principal measures are in place to motivate dealers to provide liquidity?

In many secondary government securities markets DMOs are facing liquidity problems, in particular because the willingness of many banks to be a primary dealer has decreased.[3] In many markets dealers have continued to cut back their market-making capacity. However, a recent study by the BIS Committee on the Global Financial System[4] reports that for benchmark sovereign bonds, liquidity appears little changed, although there seems to be some evidence of greater fragility in liquidity conditions. On the other hand, for some off-the-run sovereign bonds, there are some indications that the reduction in dealers' market-making capacity seems to have had a greater, adverse impact on liquidity.

Against this backdrop, this section discusses the principal measures that are in place to motivate (primary) dealers to provide liquidity. The responses to this part of the survey indicate a quite broad of practices of DMOs, ranging from no (explicit) measures (for example, Australia, Germany and Switzerland; Table 3.12) to providing various privileges, including auction fees, an exclusive mandate to be a lead manager in syndications (with accompanying fees), preferred counterparty status and (exclusive) right to participate in auctions, repo standby facilities, derivative transactions, MTN issues, buybacks and exchanges (e.g. Hungary, Italy, Poland, Spain; UK; Table 3.12).

Table 3.12. **Main measures in place to motivate dealers to provide liquidity**

	Principal measures in place to motivate dealers to provide liquidity Country-by country overview
Australia	No explicit measures are in place, although participation in syndications is based on factors including the ability to make tight two-way prices in the secondary market and distribution capabilities.
Austria	Liquidity is measured and monitored on a daily basis (on a real-time or near-real-time basis). Most prominent metrics that are used include bid/offer spreads; bid/offer sizes; quotation time; and turnover. To that end, the data from a variety of different platforms are aggregated using a scoring system.
Belgium	A ranking is constructed using the performance regarding quotations and volumes traded on selected e-platforms. The 5 primary dealers with the highest average are entitled to have access to the special non-competitive subscriptions (i.e. at the weighted average price of the auction, one week after the competitive part of the auction). Providing liquidity through market making is one of the criteria in the overall evaluation of primary dealers. Other measures include successful bidding at auctions, distribution of bonds among investors and some qualitative considerations.
Canada	Government securities distributors (GSD) who achieve a certain threshold of activity in the primary and secondary markets can be considered to have Primary Dealer (PD) status. This status enables the GSD to bid for a certain amount of each auction, among other things.
Chile	Measures include legal modifications to make possible the implementation of systems such as Euroclear so as to attract foreign investor to the market for local securities.
Czech Republic	According to the Primary Dealer Agreement, PDs are obliged to quote the prices of benchmark bonds, subject to minimum trading volumes and competitive spreads, at least 5 hours a day.
Denmark	By meeting specific obligations, primary dealers in government bonds have the following rights or privileges: 1) Participation in openings of new government bonds issues, subsequent auctions and tap-sale. 2) Participation in buy-backs and switches and to be a counterparty (insofar these operations can be conducted on the chosen platforms). 3) Using the securities lending facilities of the central government and the Social Pension Fund (as stipulated in the "Terms for the Central-Government's and the Social Pensions Fund's Securities Lending Facilities"). Primary dealers are evaluated on an ongoing basis using various indicators. The evaluation constitutes an overall assessment, including both quantitative and qualitative elements such as turnover in the secondary market, quoted bid-ask spreads, participation in auctions and quality of advisory services. Denmark does not pay the primary dealers for their services making the evaluation process less strict than when fees would be paid. (However, when the Danish government issues foreign currency bonds through syndication, the participating banks are being paid a fee.)
Finland	Finland has a seven-dimensional scorecard to measure primary dealer performance, including interdealer market making and trading (i.e. proving liquidity to investors). The Finnish DMO provides weekly reporting of realised bid-offers spreads in the interbank market, with follow-up and feedback to banks when target spreads are not met.
France	The primary dealers' agreement includes a clause by which primary dealers commit to provide liquidity in the secondary market. Their participation in the secondary market is monitored and taken into account in the annual ranking of primary dealers, which is published on our website with much publicity.
Germany	There are no specific privileges or benefits in place.
Hungary	Primary dealers have an obligation to quote two-way prices on the secondary market, and to reach at least a 3 percent share at auctions. In return, PDs have the following rights or privileges. Exclusive participation in auctions, non-competitive tenders, buy-backs, and switches. Moreover, PDs are being paid auction fees, the exclusive right to lead EUR and USD syndications and the exclusive right to participate in the stand-by repo facility operated by AKK.
Iceland	The Treasury pays each primary dealer a commission calculated as its share on the NASDAQ Iceland Exchange. The total available amount for all primary dealers is decided by the Treasury on annually basis.
Ireland	Primary Dealers are required to quote for 5 hours a day in a size of [euro] 5m on one electronic platform, at market levels. Only Primary Dealers can participate at auctions and have access to repos. Participation in syndicated transactions is available depending on their performance.

Table 3.12. **Main measures in place to motivate dealers to provide liquidity** *(cont.)*

	Principal measures in place to motivate dealers to provide liquidity Country-by country overview
Israel	Primary dealer are required to participate on a regular basis in both the primary market (auctions) and the secondary market (MTS). In return, they are entitled to a few privileges: 1) The Ministry of Finance earmarks at least 66% of all issuance amounts (in auctions) for primary dealers. 2) Access to the government bond's lending facility. 3) Eligibility for the non competitive auctions (Green Shoe), determined by the weekly ranking which, in turn, is based on the performance of primary dealers in the secondary market (in accordance with the Rules for Ranking Primary Dealers).
Italy	The main duties of primary dealers are 1) to provide trading volumes (liquidity) in the secondary market and 2) to participate in bond auctions. The status of being a primary dealer has the following privileges: i) the exclusive right to carry the title of primary dealer ii) privileged access for consulting the Italian debt management office; iii) and the right to participate exclusively in supplementary placements of debt auctions as well as exchange and buyback transactions. Moreover, PDs also enjoy exclusivity in the selection process for lead managers of syndicated deals (in euro and under the USD benchmark programme). PDs also enjoy preferential treatment in the participation in MTN issues and derivative transactions. The Italian DMO compiles an annual list with a ranking of the top five PDs (or Specialists in Italian government securities).
Japan	Preparation of so-called "Auctions for Enhanced-Liquidity" in order to maintain and enhance the liquidity of government bond markets by the additional issuance of i) "Off-the-run Bonds" and ii) "Non-Price Competitive Auctions I&II" for primary dealers.
Korea	Primary dealers have the exclusive right to participate in the primary market and receive incentives such as non-competitive purchase options. However, their designation as PDs can be suspended or cancelled when their performance do not meet the criteria set by the issuer.
Luxembourg	None
Mexico	The Federal Government implemented in 2000 the Programme for Market Makers (MM). To date, eight financial institutions are participating in this programme. They are ranked according to their performance in both the primary and secondary government securities market. This ranking is important for these MM institutions since they are used to compute the total fees they are granted for their participation in several transactions executed by the Federal Government, such as the syndicated issuances of new benchmark bonds.
Netherlands	There are quotation obligations in place. Each business day, Primary Dealers (PDs) have to quote Dutch bonds for more than 6 hours within a pre-determined bid/ask range. The daily scores are collected and each month the DMO calculates quotation scores. If a PD score is above a certain threshold, then the PD earns the right to participate in non-competitive subscriptions for the auctions in the following month. When liquidity is bad, fewer PDs are able to score above the threshold and the DMO can take appropriate measures (as it sees fit).
New Zealand	In recent years, new bonds have been launched by syndication. Appointments to the syndicate panel are based on evaluating criteria such as activity in the primary and secondary market and support for NZ government bonds. In a similar fashion, intermediaries that support the market may benefit from other business (e.g., FX and derivatives) and NZDMO or Ministerial presentations and/or attendance at conferences.
Norway	Primary dealers have access to a repo facility.
Poland	Primary Dealers are selected through a competition process that lasts 12 months. There are 3 criteria which are taken into account when assessing the performance of candidates to become PDs. The main one is their performance in the secondary market. It is measured by a specially designed "quality quotation index", calculated using an algorithm which comprises spread, volume and quoting time (in particular for Treasury Securities – TS), taking into account appropriate reference values (key modelling feature: the tighter the spread, the higher the score of the PD). Banks that are selected as PDs have many privileges, including the exclusive right to participate in primary auctions in the domestic TS market, privileges in managing issuances on foreign markets for the Ministry of Finance, etc. (For more info see the Rules and Regulations Governing the Activities of the Treasury Securities Dealer as of 12 September 2014 at *www.finanse.mf.gov.pl/c/document_library/get_file?uuid=e15d1d9a-0188-4c87-960c-d58721d6febb&groupId=766655*)
Portugal	Portugal has a primary dealership model where the performance of primary dealer banks in secondary market is being evaluated and where banks with a better performance receive higher scorings. Banks with good scores are allowed to participate in syndicated deals and derivative transactions. These measures, which have as central purpose to increase liquidity in the secondary market, can be divided into four different groups or situations: 1) Market Making Compliance (secondary market making quoting size of at least EUR 5 million in interdealer platforms for a minimum of 5 hours a day, in which the bid-offer spread cannot exceed more than 50% of the average of all quotes from all primary dealers). 2) PDs that go beyond minimum size and quotation time, thereby gaining extra evaluation points. These features were introduced for the 2015 Primary Dealership evaluation. 3) Market Making Compliance Adjusted for Volatility. In order to mitigate or cushion the lack of liquidity in very volatile market days, which will make that day even more volatile due to the lack of banks providing liquidity, we introduced in 2015 a measure that basically increases the points that banks receive in high volatility days. Clearly, highly volatile days generate more points than days with low volatility, thereby increasing the incentives for banks to quote and provide liquidity in more volatile situations. 4) Turnover with end investors: Banks receive points accordingly to the turnover made with end investors.
Slovak Republic	No measures are in place to motivate dealers to provide liquidity, except an evaluation for calculating rankings. There is a plan to introduce a dedicated electronic platform for the secondary market.

Table 3.12. **Main measures in place to motivate dealers to provide liquidity** *(cont.)*

	Principal measures in place to motivate dealers to provide liquidity Country-by country overview
Slovenia	The DMO calculates a performance index, which includes measuring secondary local currency bond market activity by Primary Dealers. This performance index is the most important factor when awarding a mandate to Primary Dealers to lead a syndicated bond issue of the Republic.
Spain	The Spanish Treasury provides an incentive scheme implemented on the basis of legislation (2012 Primary Dealers Resolution). Primary Dealers are rewarded both for their performance in primary and secondary markets. A good performance is being rewarded by allowing participation in syndications for the Kingdom of Spain as well as by providing access to the 2nd round of SPGB and *"Letras"* auctions (up to 24%, depending on the PD performance.
Switzerland	No measures are in place to motivate dealers to provide liquidity.
Turkey	Primary Dealers are obliged to promote liquidity in the secondary market. To achieve this, Primary Dealer should quote on every trading day, and on an continuous basis, bid and offer prices for benchmark securities.
United Kingdom	The DMO has limited tools to motivate dealers to provide liquidity – but can set in place an issuance programme and associated market infrastructure to facilitate the willingness and ability of dealers to provide liquidity. Privileges available to Primary Dealers include eligibility to submit competitive bids directly to the DMO, preferred counterparty status, participation in consultation meetings and eligibility for selection as a syndication Lead Manager (with accompanying fees). In general though, client demand for a service in UK Government bonds, plus the reputational and marketing benefits to PDs' banks is sufficient motivation.

Source: Responses to the 2015 survey on liquidity in secondary markets for governments bonds by OECD Working Party on Debt Management.

Measures to assess primary dealer performance differ across jurisdiction. Several OECD debt managers measure and monitor liquidity on a frequent basis, making ongoing evaluations (occasionally in real-time or near-real-time data). Metrics include: bid/offer spreads; bid/offer sizes; quotation time; turnover. Data sources include various platforms with information aggregated within scoring systems (e.g. Austria, Finland; Denmark, Poland, Portugal; Table 3.12)

Some DMOs (like the UK) argue that the available privileges should be considered as limited tools to motivate dealers to provide liquidity – but that they can set in place an issuance programme and associated market infrastructure to facilitate the willingness and ability of dealers to provide liquidity. But the UKDMO also observes that, in general, client demand for a service in government bonds, plus the reputational and marketing benefits to PDs' banks is sufficient motivation. This latter general consideration probably plays also a role in markets where DMOs report that there are no specific privileges or incentives in place.

3.12. Overview of other (additional) measures to enhance liquidity

As noted in the previous section, many DMOs are facing liquidity problems in their secondary government securities markets. Many markets dealers have continued to cut back their market-making capacity with an adverse impact on liquidity.

Against this backdrop, this section discusses other (additional) measures implemented by DMOs to boost liquidity. These actions are on top of the principal measures put in place to motivate dealers to provide liquidity as described in the previous section.

These additional measures include buy backs of illiquid lines, larger benchmark lines, a strips programme, the use of a lender of last resort facility, etc. (see Table 3.13 for a country by country overview). For example, the Danish DMO has implemented 5 measures to enhance liquidity (Table 3.13): 1) The issuance of benchmark series; 2) buy-backs 3) switch operations; 4) a securities lending facility; and 5) a price-quoting system on NASDAQ OMX.

DMOs support liquidity by implementing predictable and transparent policies (Table 3.13). For example, by using regular auction schedules or calendars (e.g. Australia,

Table 3.13. Additional measures to enhance liquidity

	Other measures in order to enhance liquidity Country-by country overview
Australia	Lender of last resort facility, regular issuance, large benchmark lines.
Austria	Existing issues are regularly tapped via monthly auctions. A strip programme is in place and can be used by investors. Benchmark issuances are executed on a regular basis, with a set auction calendar. Buybacks are taking place occasionally (on a case-by-case basis).
Belgium	The Belgian DMO uses syndications to issue new OLO lines of sufficient size. OLO lines are tapped following a predictable auction calendar, thereby further increasing the outstanding sizes (and liquidity) of the different OLO lines. There is a buy-back programme for bonds when their remaining life to maturity is 12 months. The Treasury can decide to change this maturity period but with prior notice to its primary dealers. All fixed coupon OLOs can be stripped. Since a few years all strips are fungible (interest and capital). This new feature has also increased the attractiveness (and liquidity) of the OLO lines.
Canada	The Government of Canada strives to maintain transparent, regular and diversified borrowing programmes to support liquid and well-functioning securities market: 1) The Government of Canada announces the *bond auction schedule* prior to the start of each quarter and seeks dealers' recommendations before publishing details for each operation in a call for tender in the week leading up to the auction. 2) *Benchmark target range sizes* are planned and are announced at the beginning of each fiscal year as part of the Debt Management Strategy. *Securities Lending Program*: The Bank of Canada supports the liquidity of Government of Canada securities by providing a secondary and temporary source of securities to the market through the Securities-Lending Program. Under this program, securities will be made available when the Bank believes that they are trading at the minimum bid rate or higher (in terms of spread below the target rate), or are unavailable. *Bond buyback operations "on a switch basis"*: These operations involve the exchange, on a duration-neutral basis; of less liquid bonds for building benchmark bonds and have the benefit to reduce participants' market risk at repurchase operations. These operations help build larger benchmark bonds and provide liquidity point to the market. *Bond buyback operations "on a cash basis"*: These operations are conducted shortly after a bond auction (20 minutes) and involve the exchange of less liquid or off-the-run bonds for cash. These operations help maintain larger auction sizes. However, these operations have not been used recently.
Chile	The DMO is analysing the possible implementation of a bond exchange programme that involves buying illiquid lines and issuing greater amounts of existing benchmarks. The objective is to construct a liquid yield curve by having appropriate benchmark amounts at the most important maturities.
Czech Republic	Buy-Backs, switches, benchmark issuance, flexible auction schedule, strips, lending of last resort facility.
Denmark	The Danish Debt Management Office is using various measures to enhance liquidity, including: 1) issuance in benchmark series; 2) buy-backs; 3) switches; 4) securities lending facility; 5) price-quoting system on NASDAQ OMX. The buy-back policy aims at smoothing the redemption profile and ensuring an efficient market for government bonds. *Buy-backs* can involve all domestic and foreign securities (although generally not key on-the-run issues. Buy-backs may take place via auctions, on tap or via switch auctions. The *switch facility* gives market participants the opportunity to exchange existing government securities for new, on-the-run securities at market prices. The timing of switches is demand driven. This means that switch operations do not take place regularly. The *securities lending facility* is meant for on-the-run securities and government securities with a benchmark status. For other Danish government securities collateral is required. The DMO has established with four banks a *price-quoting system* on NASDAQ OMX. This price-quoting system gives investors ongoing access to pre-trade information for Danish government securities.
Finland	New euro benchmark lines have as requirement a minimum of EUR 3 billion outstanding.
France	France has a regular monthly auction schedule: long term bonds (7-year or more) every 1st Thursday of the month; medium term (2-year to 7-year); and inflation-linked bonds every 3rd Thursday of the month. Between 2 and 4 lines are tapped or issued at each auction. There is the regular issuance of new benchmarks as well as the use of tap lines, taking into account the demand expressed by primary dealers. August and December are optional issuance months. There is a buyback programme to smooth the redemption profile. This programme allows the buying back of bonds with a maturity up to 2-years. Stripping of French bonds is allowed.
Germany	Measures to enhance liquidity include 1) a high issuance volume (in 2015 a planned funding volume of around USD 215 billion; 2) a well-established and credible issuance policy by using annual and quarterly issuance calendars that are highly transparent; 3) market support by using the option to retain at each auction a portion of securities for secondary market operations that can be sold subsequently in the secondary market; 4) offering additional investment opportunities by means of a strip programme for 10-year and 30-year Bunds; and 5) a fully established nominal and real yield curve.
Hungary	Measures include the use of a regular auction calendar and the issuance of benchmark bonds (the target is large benchmark sizes of USD 3-4 billion). In addition, the use of reopenings, switches, and buy-back auctions.
Iceland	Benchmark issuance and the use of a auction schedule. Moreover, buy back of illiquid lines with less than 6 months to maturity.
Ireland	Repos, benchmark issuance, quarterly auction schedule, occasional switches and buybacks.
Israel	Measures include: 1) the use of a Primary Dealership programme; 2) a monthly auction schedule, 3) the issuance of benchmark bonds; 4) switch auctions for off-the run bonds; 5) a lending facility for government bonds. The DMO is developing a repo market and a strips programme.

Table 3.13. Additional measures to enhance liquidity *(cont.)*

	Other measures in order to enhance liquidity Country-by country overview
Italy	The DMO uses exchange auctions and reopening of off-the-run bonds. Structural measures of a general nature include the issuance of benchmarks and the use of a calendar for regular auctions. There is also a programme for stripping both nominal and inflation linked bonds.
Japan	Measures include: 1) a buy-back programme; 2) the use of reopenings; 3) a stripping programme; 4) the annual publication of a funding plan for JGBs and 5) the announcement of auctions about three months in advance.
Korea	Various measures to enhance liquidity are in place, including: buy-backs, switches, strips, benchmark issuance and annual or monthly announcements of issuance plans.
Luxembourg	None
Mexico	Liquidity measures include the issuance of new benchmarks for *MBonds* and *Udibonos* using syndications. The issuance size of these benchmarks amount to USD 1 billion so that they can be included in global indices.
Netherlands	The DMO offers a demand driven repo facility to Primary Dealers (PDs). The PDs can use an emergency back-up facility which costs 25 bps for regular market trades. The facility provides the PDs with the possibility to cover their shorts. The DMO has not observed any significant increase in use of this facility during the last few months.
New Zealand	Measures to enhance liquidity include 1) Buy-backs for bonds approaching maturity that have a considerable amount on issue. 2) Predictable pattern of issuance – typically launch bond via syndication, blackout period for several months, regular tender programme. 3) Three-month tender schedule is announced at the end of the preceding quarter. This announcement includes tender dates, bond maturities, and volumes. 4) Preference to issue in the domestic market over foreign market (assuming no price differentiation), in order to maintain liquidity as forecast issuance declines. 5) Ongoing relations with investors and intermediaries.
Poland	Increasing the liquidity of bond market is a major objective of the Debt Management Strategy. The DMO pursues the policy of issuing i) large series of benchmark bonds on the domestic (TS) market (sizes of at least EUR 5 billion for medium- and log-term fixed rate bond series) as well as ii) large liquid bonds in the EUR and the USD markets. Poland has been adapting the issuance policy (including sales, switches and buy-back auctions) to market circumstances, in particular by monitoring demand in different segments of the TS market. The DMO has introduced the uniform price auction format and has extended this set-up also to switches. Auctions are held on the basis of quarterly and monthly schedules. In 2014 the Ministry of Finance introduced a possibility for the BGK (a state-owned bank) to conclude Buy-Backs with banks acting as PDs (or candidate PDs). This facility supports the settlement of Treasury bonds in situations with temporary, though significant, supply-demand imbalances (that is, a temporary shortage of certain bonds in the secondary market due to demand significantly exceeding supply). This BGK facility does not act as a substitute for, or a regular supplement to, the SBB market. Instead, it is meant to function as a last resort (or backstop) when serious disruptions (manifesting themselves as problems in settling Treasury bonds) cannot be corrected by the market itself. In those cases market participants need then to approach the BGK.
Portugal	The DMO aims at the regular auctioning of bonds (mainly in current benchmarks with maturities of 5-year, 7-year, 10-year, 15-year, and 30-year) to sustain liquidity. However, quarterly or annual auction calendars are not disclosed. Usually, every year, the DMO issues a new 10-year benchmark, while tapping it throughout the year so as to satisfy investor demand. This makes it one of the most liquid segments along the yield curve. Additional measures include the buying back of low-maturity bonds and bond switches (buying back low-maturity bonds and issuing long-term ones).
Slovak Republic	Benchmark issuance of bonds (with size EUR 3 billion).
Slovenia	The annual funding programme states that, in principle, benchmark issues in domestic currency (using syndications) are the primary funding instrument for satisfying the borrowing needs of the central government. However, limited investor demand by European investors required the issuance of foreign currency benchmarks in 2012 and 2013 (3 USD bond lines were issued). In March 2014, the government regained access to the European market and since then has been issuing EUR denominated bonds. An auction calendar is used for T-Bill issuance. The annual funding programmes also includes the use of buy-backs and switches. The DMO uses these liability tools based on prevailing market conditions. Buy-backs and switches were not used in 2012. In 2013, 18th month T-bills with original maturity in June 2013 were bought back in mid-April, while in July 2015 a bond with original maturity in February 2016 was exchanged for two bonds due in 2017 and 2019.
Spain	The DMO follows a benchmark issuance policy to support longer-term liquidity for bonds. Its auction schedule is liquidity-driven. In essence, Spain's debt management policy has adopted liquidity as one of the main intermediate variables. In order to improve liquidity of certain "off the run" coupon bonds, the Treasury has the option of organising special auctions. The combination of regular and special auctions provides the Treasury with more flexibility to manage its issuance operations, thereby reducing secondary market volatility around auctions. The DMO argues that the use of buy backs for illiquid lines is not the preferred technique. It can result in illiquidity costs for the public sector's balance sheet. The same can be argued (to some extent) regarding the use of switches. Nonetheless, the DMO uses from time to time switches (usually guided by other considerations than illiquidity costs). The most recent bond switch took place in June 2014, when investors were offered the opportunity to switch SPGBs maturing in 2015 into the new 10 year "Obligacion" maturing in October 2024, thereby facilitating the reinvestment of maturing bonds in 2015.

Table 3.13. **Additional measures to enhance liquidity** *(cont.)*

	Other measures in order to enhance liquidity Country-by country overview
Switzerland	Secondary market trading in Confederation bonds is supported by regularly re-opening outstanding bonds. In the important maturity range of one-to-13 years, the Confederation aims at a minimum total outstanding volume per bond line of approximately 2 billion Swiss Francs; this volume can then be further increased up to the time of maturity. In order to limit refinancing risk and to smooth the maturity profile, bond volumes at maturity should be in the region of around 6 billion. The DMO can bridge temporary illiquidity in certain bond lines by selling so-called own tranches directly to investors (on demand and at market prices).
Turkey	The Treasury uses a benchmark issuance strategy together with a set auction schedule. The market is supported by regular re-openings so as to increase the nominal stock of each security. Moreover, all coupons can be stripped.
United Kingdom	The gilt issuance programme is complemented by a supplementary programme of syndications which are flagged in advance, and mini-tenders to address pockets of particular demand.

Source: Responses to the 2015 survey on liquidity in secondary markets for governments bonds by OECD Working Party on Debt Management.

Austria, Belgium, Canada, France Germany, Ireland, Iceland, Israel, Italy, Japan, Korea, New Zealand, Norway, Poland, Slovenia, Turkey, UK, USA). Many DMOs are using buyback programmes to smooth debt redemption profiles, thereby enhancing liquidity. Liquidity is also supported by the regular issuance of (new) benchmarks, the use of tap lines (taking into account the demand preferences expressed by primary dealers) as well as by securities lending facilities.

3.13. Final comment on the potential impact of new regulations on secondary market operations

Debt managers (and market participants) have expressed concerns that some of the regulatory changes in response to the global financial crisis may have an adverse (direct) impact on liquidity in secondary markets for government bonds, leading to a likely rise in borrowing costs. In particular, DMOs have expressed concerns that lower liquidity in secondary markets is likely to affect primary market issuance in the form of a rise in borrowing costs. Some countries have argued that the Liquidity Ratio (LR) as well as the Net Stable Funding Ratio (NFSR) requirements under Basel III may have a negative impact on demand for government securities. The requirements may restrict warehousing as well as market making. Additionally, these requirements may have a negative impact on the Repo market and thus a negative impact on the functioning of secondary markets.

However, some market participants have suggested that liquidity requirements and requirements for collateral resulting from new developments in regulatory frameworks, such as the Liquidity Coverage Ratio standard under Basel III, as well as reforms to the over-the-counter derivatives market, have increased demand for government securities.

Notes

1. The missing countries are Greece, Sweden, and the United States. The Government of Estonia has not issued any securities since June 2002; therefore, Estonia has no outstanding governmental bonds. The debt portfolio of the State Treasury consists entirely of a loan from the EIB.
2. These countries are France, Japan, Luxembourg, New Zealand, Ireland, Australia, Norway and Switzerland.
3. John Geddie (2016), Squeezed bank dealers quit European government bond markets, January 21, Reuters.
4. Committee on the Global Financial System (2016), *CGFS Papers* No. 55, Fixed income market liquidity, BIS.

OECD Sovereign Borrowing Outlook 2016

Chapter 4

Transparency of public debt: Statistics, operations and policies

Drawing on the work of the OECD Task Force on Transparency of Debt Statistics, Operations and Policies, this chapter examines growing importance of transparency for public debt management and the benefits that increased transparency can bring. Enhanced transparency of strategies, operations and policies for public debt management reduces investor uncertainty, thereby increasing the attractiveness of government bond markets. This in turns broadens the investor base, lowers risk premiums and decreases borrowing costs. The chapter focuses on six areas – indicators and measures for central government debt; gross borrowing measures; indicators and measures for public debt management strategies; methods for duration and maturity calculations; and measures for roll-over risk – and offers concrete recommendations to those managing government debt.

4.1. Introduction and overview: The growing importance of transparency for public debt management

The growing importance of transparency is a worldwide trend. Transparency is linked to accountability, the disclosure of policies, accounting standards and markets. Greater transparency in sovereign debt management refers in particular to i) the institutional set-up and formulation of the public debt management strategy (including borrowing operations, funding decisions and setting the risk profile of the outstanding stock of debt) and associated policies; ii) primary public debt market operations and iii) the functioning of secondary public debt markets.

This chapter* is mainly based on the work of the OECD *ad hoc* Task Force on Transparency of Debt Statistics, Operations and Policies. Some of the transparency practices mentioned by members of the Transparency Task Force (TTF)[1] represent country-specific situations. These partly reflect the specific structure of debt portfolios in individual countries, as well as local market and policy conventions (and possible other idiosyncrasies). However, Task Force Members also suggested several general lessons and good practices regarding operations, markets and policies. They constitute the basis for recommendations or policy conclusions regarding (enhanced) transparency in seven specific policy areas (see next Section 4.2).

Key findings

- Since the onset of the global financial and economic crisis and the associated huge increase in sovereign borrowing operations, DMOs have come under additional pressures from investors and other stakeholders to increase the transparency of their operations and policies.
- Transparency in debt management operations enhances credibility, accountability and predictability. In turn, this contributes to market efficiency and lower borrowing costs. However, maximum transparency may not be the ideal strategic objective for a DMO, due to the potential for reduced flexibility and overly-complex information.
- TTF's analysis of current data dissemination practices highlight the importance of adopting common standardised measures and indicators as well as regular and timely publication of central government debt statistics.

* This chapter is based on "Suggestions, Conclusions and Recommendations by Members of the OECD Task Force on Transparency of Debt Statistics, Operations and Policies", edited by Hans J. Blommestein and Thomas Olofsson. However, the recommendations, suggestions and conclusions represent the views of individual Task Force members in their personal expert capacity. Hence, they do not convey the official views of the OECD, its member countries, or the debt management offices and other officials involved in the work of the Working Party on Public Debt Management (WPDM). The Transparency Task Force consists of the following members: Thomas Olofsson (Chair; DMO, Sweden); Wendy Chang (Central Bank, Canada); Ove Jensen (DMO/Central Bank, Denmark); Sturla Palsson and Hafsteinn Hafsteinsson (Central Bank, Icelandes); Fatos Koc (Treasury, Turkey); Hans Blommestein and Perla Ibarlucea Flores (OECD).

- TTF stresses that debt managers give careful consideration to intelligibility and accessibility features when disclosing information regarding debt statistics, operations and policies.

Additional pressures to increase the transparency of operations, markets and policies

The recent global crisis has created new challenges for Debt Management Offices (DMOs) due to a surge in borrowing requirements, relatively high debt ratios, higher rollover risk, a more challenging issuance climate with changes in borrowing procedures and funding strategies, an increase in the issuance of state guarantees, the impact of new regulations on liquidity in government bond markets, the influence of new, more complex electronic trading systems and its impact on the behaviour of primary dealers, etc. (Blommestein, Hans J., 2010).

In this challenging new environment, transparency and predictability[2] remain crucial to debt management strategies, policies and operations. In fact, the above mentioned challenges have enhanced the intrinsic need for greater transparency. For example, the rapid growth of contingent debt implies a need for increased transparency with respect to government guarantees issued.

Transparency is an issue that touches all players and institutions involved in the management, issuance and administration of public debt: DMOs, Parliaments, Minister of Finances, Central Banks, regulators and supervisors, markets, investors, rating agencies, the media and the general public. This means that the allocation of responsibilities and objectives for public debt management should be publicly disclosed and clearly explained. Moreover, transparency and accountability in the area of sovereign liability management needs to be supported by an adequate legal framework (including financial legislation) and clearly defined budget practices and public accounting standards.

Transparency in primary market procedures and techniques is essential if government borrowing costs are to be contained. In this context it is crucial that all potential buyers of government securities are provided simultaneously with the same information, and that dealers and investors are treated fairly and equally. Common standards are an essential component of enhanced transparency. For example, the Transparency Task Force recommends the adoption of a common method for the measurement and reporting of gross borrowing needs based on the methodology proposed by Blommestein, Jensen and Olofsson (2010).

Auctions are the most commonly used tool by sovereign issuers in the OECD area. This issuance technique allows for a high level of transparency supported by the timely and frequent publication of auction calendars and the prompt dissemination of auction results.

Transparency in secondary market pricing is important for liquid and efficient government securities markets. To ensure price transparency, all trades – including OTC transactions – should require centralised reporting via an exchange, a Central Securities Depository (CSD), or an industry association, that disseminates information publicly and efficiently.

DMOs with a relatively high degree of operational autonomy, and supported by highly transparent and predictable policies in both primary and secondary markets, are well placed to act as professional market players and to fulfil their mandate to minimise borrowing costs.

Against this backdrop, the Transparency Task Force[3] decided to focus on the need for (additional) transparency in the following seven specific areas:

i. Indicators and measures for central government debt;

ii. Gross borrowing measures and the link to funding needs and cash borrowing requirements;

iii. Indicators and measures for public debt management strategies;

iv. Duration and maturity calculation methods, which convey key information on the characteristics of the outstanding stock of sovereign debt;

v. Measures for roll-over risk, which have become a key focus after the start of the financial and economic crises;

vi. The use of derivatives is a key tool for managing risk exposures, while subject of a sometimes sensitive debate when it comes to articulating an optimal transparency framework;

vii. Contingent liabilities, in particular guarantees.

What are the benefits of increased transparency in government debt management?

Enhanced transparency of strategies, operations and policies for public debt management reduces investor uncertainty, thereby increasing the attractiveness of government bond markets. This in turns broadens the investor base, lowers risk premiums and decreases borrowing costs.

Other, more specific, reasons for DMOs to re-assess the need for greater transparency include the following: i) the need for DMOs to pay greater attention to roll-over risk; ii) a more challenging issuance climate;[4] iii) the necessity to stay informed about the (potential) impact of new financial regulations on the behaviour of primary dealers in primary markets and pressures on liquidity in secondary government bond markets; iv) DMOs are obliged to stay abreast about the influence of new, usually more complex, electronic trading systems on the functioning of bond markets; v) DMOs also need to pay more attention to investor relations and communication strategies; and vi) the strong increase in the issuance of latent government debt (mostly in the form of state guarantees).

Transparency and predictability are linked to openness about policies, strategies, as well as debt management operations. This in turn reflects the need for greater accountability as more transparency echoes greater demand in society for openness often expressed via a more critical attitude (by markets, regulators, rating agencies and the general public). As noted, greater transparency may lead to lower borrowing costs. For example, when investors understand better how and why decisions about changes in funding and debt management are made, uncertainty may be reduced, leading, in turn, to lower borrowing costs.

Greater accountability and transparency may contribute to (*de facto* or *de jure*) increased operational autonomy for debt management operations. In addition, more transparency about risk guidelines contributes to a better assessment of the performance of DMOs. Disclosure of risk-adjusted performance indicators, in turn, has enhanced the credibility of debt managers.

Should debt managers pursue maximal transparency?

In spite of these benefits, the argument that maximal transparency needs to be pursued under all circumstances, needs to be qualified. Clearly, a highly transparent issuance environment is highly beneficial for benchmark government bonds. However, a highly transparent environment in the case of illiquid bonds or derivatives transactions could potentially create difficulties, including attempts at market manipulation. In these situations one has to be alert for the possibility that a very high degree of transparency may move prices in a disadvantageous direction from the perspective of debt managers or investors.

This possible adverse reaction in opaque markets raises the need for determining the optimal degree of transparency rather than pursuing maximal transparency at all costs. This perspective relates to the policy question how much detail on future activities should be communicated by debt managers to market participants when they announce to pursue more transparent policies and operations. For example, sharing too detailed issuance plans with market participants could reduce the flexibility of future operations to such a degree that a particular (high) level of transparency is being perceived as unhelpful by DMOs. Hence, debt managers need to assess how much transparency they wish to follow regarding future activities and policies as regards issuance plans, buy-back operations, use of liquidity buffers, disaster recovery scenarios, etc.

Against this backdrop, it can be quite helpful to aim for more transparent policies and operations by using common definitions, measures and statistics. For example, the publication of standardised measures of central government debt (stock measures) and cash borrowing requirements (flow measures) can be expected to increase transparency. Since the risk dimension of stock and flow measures is of great importance for debt managers, standardised risk indicators need to be employed as well. Also the greater use of (more) standardised measures for both derivatives operations, as well as the issuance and management of contingent debt, are to be recommended from the perspective of greater transparency.

Clearly, the use of standardised measures makes them more easily comparable across countries while it would make the underlying policies and operations more understandable or intelligible.

4.2. Transparency of central government debt measures and indicators

Sections 4.5-4.8 discuss definitions and measures of central government debt by presenting proposals to increase the transparency of central government debt in terms of calculating and making public its overall size, as well as its composition in terms of (the characteristics of) the (issued) securities.[5] The Swedish case is used by way of illustration of several proposed or suggested transparency proposals.

When publicly available data on central government debt is not based on a common standard[6], then both aggregate figures and their constituent parts are difficult for outsiders (e.g. investors) to comprehend. For this reason, there is strong and wide support for increasing the need for better financial reporting in the public sector based on proper common standards, including by enhancing the transparency of definitions and measures of government debt. In this context, recommendations have been made by the International Federation of Accountants (IFAC) for enhanced public sector reporting, transparency and accountability by adopting International Public Sector Accounting Standards (IPSAS).[7]

National statistical offices and international agencies usually compile and publish data on general government debt using the SNA (System of National Accounts) methodology. General government debt mirrors the overall structure of the government sector. It is defined in the SNA as being composed of three parts: i) central government, ii) state and local governments and iii) social security funds.[8]

Measuring central government debt from the policy perspective of debt managers

The focus in this section is limited to making suggestions for improving the transparency of central government debt (including its composition by providing details on the range of outstanding debt instruments) guided by the policy perspective and mandate of the debt manager. Central government debt is by definition the debt raised by the DMO on behalf of the central government. DMOs are also responsible for managing and retiring central government debt.[9]

For debt managers, the common practice when it comes to transparency vis-à-vis financial markets (investors, dealers and traders) is to use and report outstanding gross nominal debt. One important reason for using face value as gross nominal debt measure is that it is the standard market practice for quoting and trading specific volumes of a particular instrument. For the same reason, DMOs are using face value when they report how much nominal debt will mature in future periods.

A second reason in favour of using face value as a measure for nominal debt is that the face value does not change except when there is a new issue of an existing instrument or the introduction of a new instrument (say with a new maturity). Changes in market values are normally of less importance for a government as a government typically does not trade its bonds.[10]

From the perspective of DMOs, reporting issuance prices seems to add little in terms of transparency. In normal circumstances, investors will be more interested in the (nominal) amount that will be paid back at redemption; this coincides of course with the original promise (and therefore contractual obligation) of the issuer.

In other words, the main purpose here is to suggest clear and transparent measures or indicators for central government debt taking into account the following considerations:

i) these debt measures are meant for use in normal circumstances (this means that there are no acute worries about default or pay-back risk and that, therefore, debt sustainability concerns are not an issue);

ii) debt indicators should support the execution of the conventional mandate of the debt manager;

iii) these debt measure or indicators are focused on central government debt (since this is by definition the debt raised by the DMO on behalf of the central government).

As explained above, the starting point is to report on total gross nominal central government debt which is defined as the sum of the face value of all instruments issued by the DMO. This is the most common measure of central government debt used by market makers, investors and DMOs under normal circumstances.

Some of the challenges faced by DMOs in measuring and reporting on central government debt portfolios with different instruments are discussed in Box 4.1.

Risk exposure of central government debt

Investors and other stake-holders have a great interest in understanding the risk exposure of central government debt. Accordingly, DMOs need to undertake risk analyses and publish the results in so-called risk reports. These reports focus on the composition of a debt portfolio, together with an assessment of the exposure of the portfolio to movements in inflation (inflation-linked bonds), exchange rates changes (hedged and unhedged bonds denominated in foreign currencies), and interest rate fluctuations (fixed versus floating debt[13]).

Box 4.1. **Reporting and measuring debt portfolios with different instruments**

Reporting on public debt portfolios and policies is quite complex. We shall illustrate some of these challenges or complications by analysing a portfolio with the following instruments: i) domestic currency debt, ii) foreign currency debt, iii) inflation-linked debt, iv) retail savings accounts, v) instruments issued for liquidity management purposes as well as vi) derivatives such as cross-currency swaps or FX forwards.

The following definitions, measures and indicators are essential for reporting on this debt portfolio with different instruments:

- **Indicator A: Nominal central government debt** is equal to the sum of the face value of all instruments (bonds and bills) issued by the DMO[11] (without taking into account the valuation effects from inflation and exchange rate movements but including the face value of instruments issued for liquidity management purposes[12]). This measure is therefore equal to the total nominal amount that needs to be paid back in the currency in which the instruments are denominated.
- **Indicator B: Uplifted value of debt** is equal to **nominal debt** using indicator A plus the valuation effects from exchange rate movements and accrued inflation-compensation.
- **Indicator C: Gross central government debt** equal to indicator B but excluding the value of instruments issued for liquidity management (when such instruments have been issued of course).
- **Indicator D:** Indicator C minus other assets of interest to investors such as on-lending to other domestic public institutions (e.g. borrowing operations by the DMO in order to increase the FX reserves of the central bank or borrowing by the DMO on behalf of state-owned companies).

Transparency about the exposure of the portfolio to fluctuations in exchange rates, inflation or interest rates is not only important for investors, but also for issuers when they create risk benchmarks.

Managing the risk exposure of the various debt categories often includes the use of derivatives as over-lay portfolios, thereby separating funding strategies from risk management. When the DMO reports on the risk exposure of central government debt, they should also make public how they are using derivatives for debt management.[14]

Table 4.1 gives an example on how to report on the risk exposure of central government debt by a DMO.

Summary recommendations and suggestions on central government debt

- Debt managers should publish on a regular basis clear and sufficiently comprehensive policy statements about the debt position of the central government, using appropriate measures and communication tools (such as web pages, newsletters, social media tools, etc.). The associated measures or indicators for central government debt should reflect the public debt strategy of the central government and its operational arm the debt management office (DMO). Adoption of these debt indicators by DMOs would support the use of common international standards, thereby strengthening the principle of transparency.
- When it comes to transparency vis-à-vis the financial market (investors, primary dealers and other traders), the common practice for debt managers is to use and report "total

Table 4.1. **Risk exposure of central government debt in Sweden**

Domestic currency debt bn		A. Nominal value	B. Uplifted value	C. Government debt	D. Extra information
	Public bonds, foreign currencies	120 944	111 940	111 940	111 940
	Other capital market debt	3 442	3 281	3 281	3 281
	Collateral	17 717	17 717	18 016	17 717
	Commercial paper, foreign currencies	42 841	42 662	42 662	42 662
	Liquidity management	-1 163	-1 160	3	-1 160
	Foreign exchange derivatives	0	85 697	85 697	85 697
	On-lending	0	0	0	-90 800
Foreign currency debt		**183 781**	**260 137**	**261 599**	**169 337**
	Inflation-linked bonds	180 530	214 794	214 794	214 794
	National debt savings	682	682	682	682
	Other capital market debt	68	83	83	83
Inflation-linked debt		**181 279**	**215 559**	**215 559**	**215 559**
	Government bonds	547 169	547 169	547 169	547 169
	T-bills	72 054	72 054	72 054	72 054
	Lottery bonds	33 356	33 356	33 356	33 356
	National debt savings	23 718	23 718	23 718	23 718
	Collateral	13 877	13 877	13 877	13 877
	Liquidity management	56 318	56 318	79 491	56 318
	Foreign exchange derivatives	0	-96 057	-96 057	-96 057
Nominal krona debt		**746 493**	**650 436**	**673 609**	**650 436**
Total debt		**1 111 553**	**1 126 132**	**1 150 767**	**1 035 332**

StatLink http://dx.doi.org/10.1787/888933393256

outstanding gross nominal debt" as an indicator in normal circumstances. The use of this debt indicator in official policy statements by DMOs is a crucial part of the communication strategy with market participants, thereby building and maintaining good investor relations.

- It is understood that other, valuable, complementary information on government debt produced or supported by international bodies or regional agencies is available. Since the work of these organisations support the adoption of international standards, they reinforce the principle of transparency. Accordingly, DMOs should be familiar with the different methodologies and standards for measuring alternative or complementary concepts of government debt (e.g. IPSAS[15]).
- The DMO should have its own publication vehicle(s). The official debt statement by the DMO should focus on measures of total central government debt that support the implementation of the core mandate of the DMO, while also providing sufficient details on its composition and risk profile. These features should be easily accessible and not be overly complex so that they are informative for other senior policymakers, parliamentarians, investors and the educated general public.
- Indicators for risk exposure (related to government liabilities) add important information. This means that also the effect of derivatives on the risk exposure of the central government debt should be included (see section 4.24 for further details).
- Information on sovereign assets associated with the management of debt (e.g. cash balances related to liquidity management) or on-lending to other government institutions such as state-owned enterprises and the central bank, are also important to investors. They should be publicly reported so as to be transparent and complete about all key public debt management operations.

4.3. Transparency of gross borrowing operations

The first step is to calculate gross borrowing requirements or needs. Total gross borrowing requirements (**GBR**) for a specific calendar year (**t = t***) refers to the volume of debt that the DMO is required to issue in order to cover (1) total redemptions within that calendar year **t*** plus (2) net cash borrowing requirements (the cash budget deficit) in **t***. In other words, the size of gross borrowing requirement in calendar year t* [**GBR(t*)**] amounts to how much the DMO needs to issue in nominal terms so as to fully pay back maturing debt plus the net cash borrowing requirement.

Total gross borrowing requirements or needs consist of gross short-term borrowing needs **[GBR(ST)]** plus gross long-term (or capital market) borrowing needs **[GBR(LT)]**.

The next step is to determine the funding strategy which involves the choice of i) money market instruments for financing **GBR(ST)** and ii) capital market instruments for funding **GBR(LT)**.

We will discuss the calculation of these components in more detail.

Net cash borrowing requirement (NCBR)

Net cash borrowing requirement (**NCBR**) in calendar year **t = t*** is equal to the central government budget deficit, measured in cash terms. This measure includes all cash flows related to the central government.[16]

NCBR may also include cash flows related to borrowing from or lending to other government institutions such as the central bank, state-owned enterprises and agencies (including what usually is referred to as on-lending).

Finally, the payments of interest are part of the **NCBR**. Interest payments would in general include both interest payments on central government debt and net interest payments on borrowing from, and lending to, other government institutions.

DMOs need also to resolve in a transparent way how to report interest payments. Are interest payments referring to gross debt only or to interest payments on gross debt minus assets associated with liquidity management.[17]

Why focus on net borrowing figures?

Investors and DMOs have a specific reason to focus on net borrowing figures (**NCBR**) and not just the gross borrowing numbers (**GBR**). One could argue that that it is easier to refinance redemptions (**TR**) as opposed to **NCBR** because it is simply a matter of rolling-over the same exposure as before (ignoring differences in time to maturity and interest rate risk in instruments being redeemed and those being newly issued). However, when net borrowing requirements are sizeable, this implies that the DMO has to sell considerable new exposure in the market.

Redemptions, buy-backs and switches

A debt management office does not only finance the NCBR but also total redemptions (**TR**). The suggested approach for calculating redemptions is a quite straight forward procedure. For calendar year **t = t*** this is the sum of all debt maturing within the upcoming calendar year **t*** or, to be more precise, redemptions within 12 months calculated from the first day of **t*** (equal to the last day of the previous calendar year).

For money market debt (with a maturity of ≤ 1 year) redemptions typically amount to the total stock of outstanding money market debt (measured at the beginning of **t = t***) as money market instruments[18] normally mature within 12 months. Hence, total money market debt redemptions calculated for total gross short-term (or money market) borrowing needs **[GBR(ST)]** are not equal to redemptions of all new money market debt issued during the calendar year **t = t***, but only redemptions of outstanding money market debt at the very beginning of the year.

Buy-backs have the same effect on gross borrowing requirements as redemptions and should therefore be accounted for in the same way. A buy-back creates a borrowing requirement. In fact, a buy-back is in many cases carried out with the purpose of creating a borrowing need thereby supporting liquidity in other (usually longer) maturities or to help investors to sell illiquid bonds with short maturities.

A switch (or an exchange) consists of two parts: a buy-back part and a new issue part. The buy-back part can therefore be treated as redemption (as discussed above) and the issue part as a regular outright issue (as part of a market-based borrowing operation). Switches are used to make it possible for the investor (and the issuer) to exchange bonds with different features; for example, exchanging two bonds with different maturities. It is suggested to treat the net of the switch (if any) as contributing to gross borrowing requirements. Simply adding the amount of all switches to total gross borrowing needs would result in an overstatement of the actual need to borrow.

Derivatives and gross borrowing needs

Derivatives are not part of the discussion on measuring gross borrowing needs as derivatives are used to change risk exposures; swaps and other derivatives are therefore not part of the funding or issuance strategy. However, maturing swaps that result in gains or losses are part of the net cash borrowing requirement (NCBR) and therefore they are part of total gross borrowing needs, GBR.

Recommendations and suggestions for measuring gross borrowing needs

- The size of gross borrowing operations is by definition equal to the amount that governments need to borrow. Gross borrowing requirements are calculated on the basis of information on i) net cash borrowing requirements and 2) redemptions (debt maturing within the upcoming calendar year). It is recommended to use a standard measure for calculating gross borrowing requirements as this enhances the transparency of borrowing or issuance operations.
- Gross borrowing operations refer to the financing of gross borrowing requirements based on a transparent (predictable) funding strategy. The funding strategy is informed principally by cost versus risk considerations. The funding or issuance strategy determines the choice of i) money market instruments for financing gross short-term needs and ii) capital market instruments for funding gross longer-term requirements. Hence, the funding strategy reflects the financing structure in terms of instruments and maturity.
- Transparent gross borrowing operations (based on agreed upon measures) are a key component of the predictability of public debt management policies because they increase the predictability of gross borrowing operations and associated funding strategy, thereby reducing the cost of borrowing.

4.4. Transparency of Government Debt Management Strategies and the Composition of Debt

The composition of the stock of debt is an important determinant for assessing the vulnerability of government balance sheets to a wide range of shocks. The structure or composition of public debt is instrumental in reducing the exposure of governments to a range of risks, including interest rate risk, currency risk and refinancing (or rollover) risk. For that reason, governments formulate targets for key "risk indicators" or, more ambitiously, construct "preferred" or "optimal" debt portfolios that mirror metrics such as preferred currency composition, preferred share of fixed-rate debt, desired duration, and favoured maturity structure of the outstanding stock of debt.[19] These "preferred" or optimal portfolios can serve as guidance for preferred debt management strategies and, accordingly, for government borrowing operations and other public debt transactions, for example, in the form of strategic benchmarks for borrowing operations.

A preferred Debt Management Strategy (DMS for short) consists of the government's objectives, borrowing plans, risk management targets and other policies for the management of its domestic and foreign debt.[20] Accordingly, DMOs formulate targets for the composition of preferred debt portfolios. Most commonly used target indicators or metrics include "Share of fixed rate debt to total debt", "Share of FX debt to total debt", "Debt maturing in 12 months (or 24-36 months)", "Debt re-fixing of interest rate within 12 months (or 24-36 months)" and "Average maturity of debt".

In recent years, DMOs have issued an increasing amount of inflation-linked bonds. As a result, the "Share of inflation-linked debt" has also become an important target indicator.

Strategic benchmarks are often set for the medium term (as part of Medium Term Debt Strategies – MTDS) with annual reviews of the actual or realised values.

The historical record shows that poorly structured sovereign debt portfolios have often been important factors triggering or exacerbating financial crises. For that reason, debt management strategies should take into account the preferred risk profile of sovereign debt portfolios. In this way, the funding strategy is an important tool for managing (limiting) the risk exposure of the stock of debt, while liquidity buffers play an important supporting role.[21]

The importance of the transparency of debt management strategies

Transparency about debt strategies makes a key contribution to the predictability of debt management operations, thereby reducing uncertainty for investors and lowering borrowing costs. In many countries the sovereign debt stock is the largest security portfolio. Hence, information about the likely future state of the composition of government debt (maturity, currency, yield, etc.) is of great significance for financial markets.

Moreover, publicly available information on portfolio targets allows financial market players such as investors and credit rating agencies to make an assessment to what extent these targets are met. Transparency of strategic benchmarks enhances therefore the credibility of DMOs, while lowering borrowing costs.[22]

Disclosure about the practices of DMOs reveals different preferences among OECD countries driven by the basic trade-off between more transparency and less flexibility. On the one hand, disclosing more details on strategic targets increases transparency. On the other hand, it reduces the flexibility of implementing funding programmes. Some DMOs attach greater value to flexibility than others. These DMOs prefer to disclose information about medium-term debt strategies without disclosing numerical targets (as opposed to DMOs that publish quantitative benchmarks). Instead of disclosing numerical targets, these DMOs publish qualitative information about the main features of the desired portfolio composition, together with information on changes in the use of instruments (e.g. the choice of FX vs local currency denominated debt, fixed vs floating rate instruments, short vs long term debt instruments).

Strategic benchmarks may also cover contingency policies such as the use of a "liquidity buffer". In recent years, the use of these buffers has been attracting increasing attention by investors and credit rating agencies, together with a positive assessment. Also here disclosure practices differ among OECD countries. Many DMOs prefer not to publish quantitative information. Instead, they disclose that they are maintaining a liquidity buffer (for rainy days) but without giving numerical details.

In sum, DMOs disclose information about debt management strategies in the form of quantitative benchmarks or qualitative statements. Disclosing quantitative benchmarks means making public numerical targets for each risk indicator. This will benefit investors and other stakeholders, while this practice makes debt management more predictable.

Publicly available information on the use of 18 debt management strategies

This section discusses the results of a Survey on the use of debt management strategies by 18 DMOs,[23] of which 14 from the OECD area, by using publicly available information on quantitative benchmarks and/or qualitative targets regarding exchange rates, interest rates, and indicators for re-financing risk and liquidity risk.

The results of this Survey among 18 DMOs (undertaken in 2014) can be summarised as follows:

- All 18 DMOs disclose on their websites information about their debt strategies as part of the overall debt management framework.
- DMSs are often published in the form of general debt management reports or via more specific (supporting) strategy documents.
- Debt strategies are typically formulated for the medium-term (3-5 years). These MTDSs are then updated and, when needed, revised annually (for example, Iceland, Canada and Turkey). Some countries only publish strategies for the coming year (e.g. Austria).
- 13 countries (Austria, Brazil, Canada, Colombia, Czech Republic, Denmark, Hungary, Iceland, Indonesia, Latvia, the Netherlands, South Africa and Sweden) publish both quantitative targets and the realised, numerical results of the associated indicators. This approach enables market players and other stakeholders to assess the performance of DMOs.
- The countries that publish quantitative benchmarks often announce numerical targets within a band so as to allow room for deviations (e.g. Brazil, Iceland, the Netherlands and Sweden). This band gives DMOs some flexibility to respond to emerging risks and/or opportunities.
- Some countries (including Germany, Italy and Turkey) prefer to disclose qualitative targets instead of numerical targets (although we understand that quantitative targets are normally formulated and monitored for internal purposes).
- The degree of transparency regarding methodologies for formulating a MTDS differs among DMOs. Some countries (such as Denmark, Colombia, Germany, the Netherlands,

Turkey and the UK) publish modelling details as part of their publicly disclosed strategic guidelines or in separate research papers. Several other countries provide only very limited information about their modelling framework and practices.

Recommendations and suggestions on the use of debt management strategies

- DMOs should use and explain strategic indicators. They should also provide information on what these medium-term strategies signify and outline the policy implications for public debt management.
- Debt managers should publish medium/long-term debt strategies so as to enhance the predictability of debt management policies and to lower borrowing costs. When actual or realised numerical results of the MTDS are published, investors, primary dealers and credit rating agencies are in a better position to make assessments about progress made within the context of publicly announced numerical strategic targets.
- In addition to strategic benchmarks regarding the composition of the debt portfolio, credible information on contingency policies (e.g. liquidity buffers) should also be made public since they provide cushions during stressful market conditions.
- Target indicators can be disclosed numerically or qualitatively. Numerical targets can be published with a band so as to allow room for some flexibility.
- Methodologies used in the calculations of quantitative indicators should be explained and published in detail in order to enhance an accurate understanding of the indicators.

4.5. Transparency of interest rate risk: Policy framework for measuring and monitoring interest rate risk

Government debt managers use various metrics to measure and monitor interest rate risk so as to identify the interest rate exposure of the government debt portfolio.

The most commonly used measures are "Macaulay duration", "modified duration", "average time to maturity" and "average time to re-fixing (ATR)" (OECD, 2005). Macaulay duration is the weighted average term to maturity of a debt instrument. It is the measurement of how long it takes for a bond to be repaid by its internal cash flows. Modified duration estimates the sensitivity of bond prices due to variations in interest rates (Cosio-Pascal, 2007). Macaulay duration is presented in years, while modified duration is expressed in percentage terms.

Duration is a summary measure, which does not contain information about the absolute size or the maturity distribution of the interest-rate exposure. For that reason DMOs also calculate "average time to re-fixing" and "share of debt re-fixed within 12 months". ATR is an interest rate risk indicator where nominal values of cash flows are used in the calculations, while present values of cash flows are used for Macaulay and modified duration calculations. The calculation of measures for market risk is summarized in Annex 4.A1.[24]

Transparency practices in selected OECD countries

To get a general idea about disclosure practices, we studied the transparency practices of DMOs in 10 countries.[25] To that end, we examined the websites of these countries in terms of publicly available information regarding duration and ATR. We also looked at i) how frequent information is made available, ii) the details of the methodologies of the various statistics and iii) which instruments in the portfolio are used for calculating the various statistics.

All 10 DMOs surveyed publish statistics for duration, ATR or ATM using external debt management reports or other publicly available documents. But there are significant differences in frequency, details provided on calculation methods and which instruments are used.

Indeed, there are remarkable differences in the release frequency of indicators of interest rate risk. Most countries publish quarterly figures, but some prefer a monthly or annual frequency. Clearly, this difference in release frequencies makes the comparison across countries more difficult.

Most countries publish time series of the various debt statistics (via external reports and/or web sites). Publishing statistics via websites allows relatively easy access, but making available meaningful information requires that sufficiently explanatory information is published as well. Unfortunately, the latter information is often lacking. For example, it is often not clear how DMOs are dealing with the ccomplexities in calculating the duration of price index-linked bonds (see Box 4.2). Moreover, it is often unclear whether swaps, inflation-linked instruments, and/or floating- rate instruments are included in the calculations. Finally, the interest rate assumptions for duration" should be clearly explained so that it is easier to analyse the interest rate exposure of the government.

Box 4.2. **Complexities in calculating the duration of price index-linked bonds**

Duration is a measure that gives an idea about the sensitivity of the price of a nominal bond to changes in nominal yields. Likewise, price index-linked bonds are typically measured with respect to real yields. Calculating the *nominal* duration for these bonds can therefore be complicated.

On the other hand, the calculation of the *real* duration for inflation linked bonds (linkers) is relatively simple by applying the duration formula used for nominal bonds. This calculation takes only the real component of each coupon and the real yields into account. This duration is a measure of the linkers' price sensitivity to changes in real yields.

In other words, real and nominal durations measure the sensitivity to different kinds of yields. But in order to ensure that a comparison is made on a *like-for-like basis*, it is not appropriate to combine index-linked and conventional bonds' duration statistics directly (Phoa, 1998). Instead, various approaches can be used to overcome this problem. The general objective of these methods is the same in the sense that the DMO calculates the nominal duration of inflation linked bonds by making appropriate assumptions so as to obtain nominal cash flows (Phoa, 1998; Fabozzi and Choudhry, 2004). In this way, index-linked bonds whose final cash flows have been fixed in nominal terms and trade with respect to nominal yields can be included in the duration calculations.

Due to these complexities, many countries choose not to include linkers in published statistics on nominal portfolio duration. However, the share of inflation-linked bonds in the government debt portfolio has increased considerably in recent years. Since this share stands around 20 percent of central government debt in several countries, consideration should be given to including linkers in portfolio calculations and make the results publicly available.

Recommendations and suggestions for measuring and monitoring interest rate risk

This section concludes and makes suggestions or recommendations for a more transparent and uniform framework for measuring and monitoring interest rate risk. Accordingly, the following suggestions or recommendations would enhance the transparency of the measurement of two key indicators: "duration" and "time-to-re-fixing":

- Publish key indicators on (at least) a quarterly basis.
- Consideration should be given to include linkers in portfolio calculations and make the results publicly available.
- Provide clear information which part of the portfolio (in terms of debt instruments) is excluded from the calculations and why.
- Explain clearly the details of the methodologies used in the calculations (for example, how the duration of inflation-linked bonds is calculated; see Box 4.2 below).
- DMOs should also include information on the interpretation of calculated statistics and their possible policy implications.
- Provide user-friendly access to current and historical figures.

4.6. The importance of the transparency of rollover risk

The risk that debt will have to be rolled over at an unusually high cost or, in extreme cases, cannot be rolled over at all, can exacerbate or even trigger a debt crisis. High rollover risk are likely to create the circumstances where investors become reluctant from buying longer-term government bonds. Instead, they may limit themselves to investing in (very) short-term paper, thereby making the debt portfolio even more vulnerable.

Improving the transparency of rollover risk[26] is likely to reduce investor uncertainty, leading to more credible debt management and lower borrowing costs.

Debt portfolio indicators that measure rollover risk play i) a *diagnostic role* for identifying vulnerabilities in the government debt structure ii) while they can also serve as an important *portfolio benchmarking role* for reducing portfolio risk.

Commonly used risk measures

The following measures, capturing the vulnerability of the debt portfolio to refinancing (or rollover) risk, are often used by DMOs:

i) the redemption profile;

ii) the ratio of debt maturing in a specific period to the total debt portfolio representing the gross exposure to rollover risk;

iii) the Average Time to Maturity (ATM) (see Annex 4.A1).

Most sovereign debt issuers make available public information on rollover risk (both past, current, and projected information). However, disclosure practices are not uniform. The following section intends to suggest or recommend best practices for the transparency of rollover risk.

Suggested recommendations on disclosing information on rollover risk

The following 4 recommendations capture the essence of disclosing information on rollover risk by DMOs. Adoption by DMOs would contribute to more uniform disclosure practices.

- Sovereigns should clearly disclose and regularly update (at least quarterly) their debt maturity profile for the next 12 months. Information on the amount of debt maturity in the short term is fundamental in assessing a country's rollover risk. It can be expressed in a number of ways, from daily maturity profile to statistics calculated at a more aggregated level.

- Sovereigns should provide regularly updated (at least quarterly) information on average term to maturity (ATM), and/or information on the composition of their debt portfolio. ATM provides a high level summary of rollover risk in the debt portfolio and its popularity allows for easy international comparison. Information on debt composition further improves investors' ability to form an assessment of a country's rollover risk.
- All debt that is issued as a funding tool should be included in the calculation of debt metrics or statistics. Moreover, the calculation methodology should be clearly stated to allow for better understanding of the figures. The intent of publishing rollover metrics and statistics is to provide information on the issuer's refinancing risk. Therefore that any debt (either domestic or foreign currency denominated) that is issued as a funding tool should be included in the calculation. However, countries may choose to exclude foreign currency denominated debt if such debt is issued solely for the purpose of funding their foreign currency reserves.
- Disclosure of reserve adequacy (liquidity buffer) improves investors' confidence and sovereigns should try to include this information as part of their regular report. The use of a liquidity buffer safeguards a sovereign's ability to meet obligations in situations where normal access to funding markets may be disrupted or delayed. Although it is not a rollover metric, providing information on a liquidity buffer (i.e. an indicator of reserve adequacy) can improve investors' confidence. For example, in Canada, the performance of its prudential liquidity plan[27] is reported in the annual Debt Management Report. Information on cash balances and foreign exchange assets is also available to the public.[28] Moreover, statistics on the plan's implementation as well as tracking of liquidity targets is provided to internal working groups on a weekly basis, and to senior management at a quarterly frequency.

4.7. Enhanced transparency and the use of derivatives by debt managers

Government debt managers are using derivatives to separate funding decisions, focused on minimising borrowing costs, from risk management, concentrated on the optimal portfolio composition. In this way, DMOs can manage the key portfolio risks (such as interest-rate risk, currency risk and refinancing risk), while separately pursuing low borrowing costs.

In many countries derivatives are an integral part of government debt management. For that reason transparency in using derivatives is of great importance for investors, rating agencies, supervisors and other stakeholders because it contributes to a better understanding and assessment of government debt policy.

Enhanced transparency also contributes to higher credibility of public debt management. For example, sufficient transparency would avoid the suspicion that debt managers and other financial policymakers are using derivatives for dubious purposes; e.g. for "window dressing" public finances such as deficit and debt figures.

Suggested recommendations on disclosing information when using derivatives

This section provides suggested recommendations for enhancing the transparency when debt managers are using derivatives. As noted, the adoption of these recommendations is likely to contribute to higher credibility of public debt policies, including those related to government borrowing operations, funding choices and risk management.

- Sovereign debt managers should clearly articulate for which strategic and operational purposes they are using derivatives. For example, the Danish DMO formulated the following policy statement about the use of derivatives:[29]

  "Government Debt Management has been using swaps for almost 30 years. Over time, the trend has gone from relatively complex swaps to plain vanilla swaps.

  Swaps are an integral part of government debt management. They are either transacted in connection with specific foreign loans or as portfolio swaps aimed at managing the overall interest-rate and currency exposure. Consequently, swaps cannot be assessed separately from the government debt portfolio.

  The use of swaps provides for more flexible debt management, allowing a more distinct separation of issuance policy and the management of interest-rate risk. The focus of the issuance policy can thus be on creating high liquidity in the bond series, building up a broad investor base and keeping the re-financing risk low."

- Sovereign debt managers should at the minimum disclose once-a-year information about new swaps that were concluded during the year and disclose portfolio details regarding swaps. DMOs should also make public information about the end-year portfolio of swaps at both nominal and market values. Table 4.2 gives an example of new interest-rate swaps concluded by the Danish DMO in 2011.

Table 4.2. **Central Government Interest Rate Swap Transactions, 2011**

Loan No.	Start date	Terminations date	Amount, million euro
Interest-rate swaps in euro			
1440	20-01-11	20-01-21	100
1444	26-01-11	26-01-21	100
1446	03-02-11	03-02-21	100
1454	08-03-11	08-03-21	100
1464	23-03-11	23-03-21	100
1465	28-03-11	28-03-21	100
1467	30-03-11	30-03-21	100
1468	05-04-11	05-04-21	100
1471	08-04-11	08-04-21	100
1476	23-05-11	23-05-21	100
1484	23-06-11	23-06-21	100
1490	01-07-11	01-07-21	100
Interest-rate swaps in euro, total			1 200

Note: The Kingdom of Denmark receives a fixed interest rate and pays 6-month Euribor on swaps transacted in 2011. No krone interest-rate swaps have been concluded in 2011.

StatLink http://dx.doi.org/10.1787/888933393263

When possible, the swap portfolio should provide detailed information about a) different instruments (interest-rate swaps, cross-currency swaps, etc.) and b) usage (portfolio swaps, liability swaps in connection to foreign loans, etc.). An example is given in Table 4.3.

- Sovereign debt managers should provide information on the characteristics of the debt portfolio before and after concluding swaps. This should be done in a transparent way and could include the following indicators; including: share of public debt in FX currency (before and after swaps); duration of public debt in domestic and FX currency (before and after swaps) and interest-rate exposure (before and after swaps).
- DMOs should publish the following indicators on how they manage counter-party risk associated with derivatives; including, information on the use of ISDA and

Table 4.3. **Central Government Swap Portfolio, end-2012**

	Number of swaps	Principal, kr. billion	Market value, kr. billion
Interest rate swaps for duration management			
Interest-rate swaps in kroner	93	25.6	2.5
Interest-rate swaps in euro	71	47.5	6.5
Swaps in connection to foreign loans			
Swaps in connection to foreign loans[1]	7	38.4	2.3
Other cross-currency swaps			
Swaps from kroner to euro	1	1.5	0.0
Swaps from kroner to dollar	23	7.5	-0.1
Total	195	120.5	11.3

1. For foreign loans in other currencies than euro, the loan proceeds are swapped to euro.

StatLink http://dx.doi.org/10.1787/888933393270

CSA-agreements for reducing counter-party risk; market value of the swap portfolio before and after collateral and information on the concentration of counterparties in the swap portfolio.[30]

Concluding comment on the transparency of using derivatives

As noted, enhanced transparency on the use of derivatives by debt managers has many advantages. However, there can be situations where there is a *trade-off* between the degree of transparency on the one hand, and the need for market confidentiality, on the other. For example, it can be desirable for governments to delay making public information about swap transactions. Otherwise, market participants could take advantage of immediately disclosed information by moving against the government and/or against counterparties (that have undertaken swap transactions with the government).

4.8. Transparency of contingent liabilities

Contingent liabilities are latent obligations that materialise when a particular, discrete event occurs. A key function of the State is to protect its citizens against major, unforeseen adverse events. For that reason, contingent liabilities feature prominently on government balance sheets. Moreover, the outstanding amount of latent or contingent debt in the OECD area has grown strongly since the outbreak of the global crisis. For these reasons, a high degree of transparency of contingent liabilities is of fundamental importance.

Two key characteristics of a contingent liability are uncertainty i) when the contingency will be triggered and ii) about their *ex ante* size (although estimates about *ex ante*, potential exposures can be made in case of explicit contingent liabilities).

Implicit and explicit contingent liabilities

Many contingent liabilities are *implicit* in the sense that they are considered moral or political obligations or (perceived) responsibilities of the government including such cases as: systemic bank failures (leading to a bail-out); failure of a non-guaranteed pension fund; municipal defaults and outlays due to a natural disaster relief and other catastrophes.

Implicit contingent liabilities are only triggered and recognised after a specific event materialises. They are therefore not identifiable *ex ante*. A discussion about (an increase in) the transparency of implicit contingent liabilities is therefore not relevant. Debates of this nature might even backfire when the market would misprice risks as a result of this "transparency dialogue".

Explicit contingent liabilities, on the other hand, are legally binding claims based on contracts that, in turn, have a basis in laws. Explicit contingent liabilities of the government may take various forms including: credit guarantees; loans guaranteed by the government such as mortgage loans and student loans, agriculture loans, etc.; civil service pensions; deposit insurance; (partially) guaranteed private investment projects; etc.

Explicit contingent liabilities can take a variety of forms, but state guarantees are the most common. For the sake of simplicity, the terms "state guarantees" and "explicit contingent liabilities" will be used interchangeably. The main focus will be on credit guarantees which are a common and simple form of state guarantee.[31]

Public-Private Partnerships (PPPs) can be regarded as a source of both explicit and implicit contingent liabilities. PPP contracts that include state guarantees need to be treated as explicit contingent liabilities. On the other hand, it is not unusual that these contracts result in unexpected government commitments that were neither anticipated nor expected; in which cases these projects become a source of implicit contingent liabilities.

How similar are state guarantees to conventional debt instrument?

State guarantees are in many ways similar to conventional debt instruments. In particular, they have to be serviced by taxpayer's money when they are called or triggered. Hence, guarantees represent a (potential) claim on the government's balance sheet. For these reasons contingent debt should be ruled by similar rules and procedures as conventional debt, including by having in place a legal framework under which such liabilities can be issued. Moreover, state guarantees are identifiable, quantifiable and, as a result, manageable. Thus, many of the principles and recommendations regarding the transparency of conventional government debt should also be applied to state guarantees.

How to disclose state guarantees?

A framework for making public state guarantees such as credit guarantees requires adequate disclosure of both qualitative and quantitative information.

Qualitative information

When communicating with bond investors, governments (in their capacity as issuers) need to provide sufficient information on how state guarantees are issued and also how they are being managed after issuance.

Such a qualitative overview includes the disclosure of the objectives of the different state guarantees, the legal framework for issuing new guarantees, the management of fees and reserves, the monitoring of outstanding guarantees, and how frequent governments disclose key information.

Disclosure can be done separately for large, specific beneficiaries such as, for example, SOEs or infrastructure projects. Or disclosure can involve making public the various guarantee programmes in the case of numerous borrowers (beneficiaries); for example, student loans programmes or mortgage loans programmes.

Quantitative information

The focus of quantitative information should be on the size of exposures, costs, and payments related to explicit contingent liabilities such as outstanding credit guarantees.

The first step is to disclose the outstanding amounts of such guarantees. As noted, it is suggested to make public such figures separately for i) specific, large beneficiaries and ii) for guarantee programmes targeting numerous, small beneficiaries (borrowers).

Where applicable, the exposure of credit guarantees can also be categorised on the basis of prominent risk factors, such as currency and interest rates. For example, the Icelandic government provides information on the exposure of State guarantees with respect to different risk factors such as exposures to currencies and interest rates.

Secondly, the transparent reporting of costs and payments are an essential part of disclosed quantitative information.

Third, expected losses (for the remaining maturity of issued guarantees) and the amount of outstanding guarantees that are likely to be triggered in the near future, should be made public as well.

Finally, information on actual cash flows related to triggered guarantees as well as collected fees and recoveries should also be released.

Reporting information on Public-Private Partnerships

Information on Public-Private Partnership (PPP) contracts should be disclosed when they are signed but also when changes are made in previously signed contracts. Crucial information to be made public concerns government commitments (guarantees) as part of PPP contracts as well as future streams of payments. Moreover, any side agreements should also be published, in particular regarding government guarantees. Rules for constructing PPP contracts should also be disclosed (including restrictions related to commercially confidential information). Information on the performance of PPP projects should be regularly published. Synopses of PPP contracts should be put together and published in plain language. These summaries should include the most important elements of the contract, including of course its main objective and government commitments.

Recommendations and suggestions on contingent public debt

State guarantees are in many ways similar to conventional debt instruments. Hence, many of the principles regarding the transparency of conventional government debt should therefore be applied in case of contingent debt.

- Governments, in their capacity as issuers, should disclose sufficient information on state guarantees, both of a qualitative and quantitative nature.
- Qualitative information should entail an overview of how state guarantees are issued and managed, as well as the objectives of these guarantees, the legal framework for issuing new guarantees, the management of fees and reserves, the monitoring of outstanding guarantees, and how frequent governments disclose key information.
- Disclosure of quantitative information should focus on the size of exposures, costs and payments related to outstanding (credit) guarantees.
- Governments should also be transparent about expected losses, the amount of guarantees that are likely to be called in the near future and records of actual cash flows.
- Finally, information on Public-Private Partnership (PPP) contracts should also be disclosed on the basis of the suggestions made in the previous section.

Notes

1. The Transparency Task Force consists of the following members: Thomas Olofsson (Chair; DMO, Sweden; central government debt indicators and measures for sovereign borrowing); Wendy Chang (Central Bank, Canada; roll-over risk); Ove Jensen (DMO/Central Bank, Denmark; derivatives); Sturla Palsson and Hafsteinn Hafsteinsson (Central Bank, Iceland; contingent liabilities); Fatos Koc (Treasury, Turkey; debt management strategies and interest rate risk); Hans Blommestein (OECD; central government debt indicators, measures for sovereign borrowing, debt management strategies and interest rate risk). Perla Ibarlucea Flores (OECD) provided overall statistical support.
2. Concepts that are linked to openness and accountability.
3. The Transparency Task Force consists of the following members: Thomas Olofsson (Chair; DMO, Sweden; central government debt indicators and measures for sovereign borrowing); Wendy Chang (Central Bank, Canada; roll-over risk); Ove Jensen (DMO/Central Bank, Denmark; derivatives); Sturla Palsson and Hafsteinn Hafsteinsson (Central Bank, Iceland; contingent liabilities); Fatos Koc (Treasury, Turkey; debt management strategies and interest rate risk); Hans Blommestein (OECD; central government debt indicators, measures for sovereign borrowing, debt management strategies and interest rate risk). Perla Ibarlucea Flores (OECD) provided overall statistical support.
4. These challenges led, in several jurisdictions, to changes in borrowing procedures and funding strategies (Hans J. Blommestein [2011], Public Debt Management and Sovereign Risk during the Worst Financial Crisis on Record: Experiences and Lessons from the OECD Area, in: Carlos A. Primo Braga and Gallina A., Vincelette [eds.], Sovereign Debt and the Financial Crisis – *Will This Time Be Different?*, The World Bank).
5. It is not always straightforward to make general recommendations as there are often country specific features that need to be taken into account.
6. The absence of a common standard is likely to result in the use of multiple definitions that are often not clearly enough explained.
7. The adoption of IPSAS implies the use of accrual-based accounting in the public sector. In this context, IFAC has recommended that the G-20 actively encourage and support the adoption of IPSAS as it reinforces the principles of transparency and allows for the monitoring of government debt for their true economic implication. To that end, the IFAC has submitted on various occasions letters to the G20 with a series of recommendations on public sector financial management, transparency, and accountability. The various letters to the G-20 with the full recommendations can be found on the IFAC website.
8. Eurostat (the European statistical agency) follows specific EU rules. The underlying definition is based on general principles as outlined in SNA93. In Europe these guidelines are specified in the ESA95 principles with additional information outlined in the EDP (Excessive Deficit Procedure). Commission Regulation No. 220/2014 of March 2014 stipulates that all references to "ESA 95"shall be replaced by "ESA 2010".
9. From the methodological perspective of the international SNA standard, the information on central government debt discussed and reported in this section from the perspective of debt managers can be considered as input for so-called *analytical or satellite accounts*. Some of this *complementary* statistical information is more detailed in terms of instruments and debt policy operations than in SNA-based reporting. Hence, the different methodologies for reporting government debt incorporate sovereign debt measures that differ in terms of scope, perspective and detail. These different measures can often be considered as complementary as their use coincides with the different perspectives and roles of issuers, investors, supervisors, etc.
10. The situation changes when there are (suspected) debt sustainability problems, followed, in serious circumstances, by a debt restructuring process.
11. The following approach is recommended in case of issuance of instruments in foreign currencies. Calculate the nominal value of the stock of FX debt in terms of domestic currency by using the exchange rate at the time of issuance. This approach makes it quite simple to include the domestic currency value of FX debt in indicator A. This calculated value constitutes also the basis for calculating exchange rate losses or gains under measure B.
12. When the DMO issues government securities for liquidity management purposes the proceeds are not (immediately) used for covering deficits. Instead, they are invested in deposits, repos or other cash management instruments. The face values (or liquidity values) of these liquidity management instruments represent therefore the amount of assets on the balance sheet of the

government. They are publicly reported so as to be transparent and complete about all public debt management operations.

13. The distinction between fixed versus floating is not related to "time to maturity" considerations. Instead, this distinction is important for assessing re-fixing risk. A Floating Rate Note (FRN) can have a very long time to maturity when issued but has the same risk exposure to changes in short-term interest rates as a T-bill.
14. See Section 4.24 for details on the reporting on the use of derivatives by DMOs.
15. International Public Sector Accounting Standards.
16. In Sweden the "budget balance" is by law defined as the net cash borrowing requirement.
17. For example, in Sweden, the interest received on assets (within the context of debt management) is taken into account in calculating total net interest payments (making it a net measure). Also, net interest payments on borrowing from, and lending to, other government institutions are included in total net interest payments in the Swedish accounting methodology.
18. Money market debt include T-bills, commercial paper and instruments used for liquidity management such as deposits, repos, etc.
19. See Annex 4.A1 for details on disclosing information on the following concepts: "*Duration*", "*Time to Re-fixing*" and "*Time to Maturity*".
20. A comprehensive, balance sheet approach would also involve the integrated (risk) management of sovereign assets. See Hans J. Blommestein and Fatos Koc (2008), Sovereign Asset and Liability Management: Practical Steps Towards Integrated Risk Management, *Forum Financier/Revue Bancaire et Financière*, 2008/6-7.
21. For example, many DMOs prefer to maintain cash balances as a cushion for stressful (funding) situations. These balances, acting as a "*Liquidity Buffer*", are formulated as part of a contingency plan with a specific benchmark for its level. Having a liquidity buffer increases the financial flexibility of sovereign issuers during stressful market conditions. This policy enhances the confidence of investors. Maintaining liquidity buffers has therefore become a widespread practice among OECD issuers, especially in the wake of the global crisis. A liquidity buffer consists of highly liquid assets (notably cash) that can be used during stressful borrowing periods. (The 2010 OECD survey on Liquidity Buffer practices in OECD countries showed that, at that time, 25 DMOs were using a liquidity buffer policy for cash and debt management purposes.)
22. Publicly available medium- and/or long-term strategic benchmarks are the key elements of a transparent MTDS. The key strategic targets usually cover interest rates, exchange rates and indicators for re-financing risk. These are published in general debt management reports and/or in other supporting strategy documents.
23. Austria, Australia, Brazil, Canada, Czech Republic, Colombia, Denmark, UK, Germany, The Netherlands, Hungary, Iceland, Indonesia, Italy, Latvia, South Africa, Sweden and Turkey.
24. These formulas are the most commonly used ones by DMOs.
25. Canada, Denmark, France, Germany, Iceland, Italy, Sweden, Turkey, UK and USA.
26. Rollover risk is another term for refinancing risk.
27. The Government of Canada's overall liquidity levels cover one month of net projected cash flow, including coupon payments and debt refinancing needs.
28. Information is available through the Fiscal Monitor and Public Accounts of Canada.
29. See *Danish Government Borrowing and Debt 2010*, Danish Central Bank.
30. This information can be provided without disclosing the names of counterparties.
31. A credit guarantee is a contract where the government takes over the credit risk of the lender in case the borrower fails to honour his/her obligations. See Hans J. Blommestein (ed.), 2005, Advances in Risk Management of Government Debt, Organisation for Economic Co-operation and Development.

References

Blommestein, Hans J. (2010), "Responding to the crisis: Changes in OECD government debt issuance procedures, portfolio management and primary dealer systems", *OECD Journal: Financial Market Trends*, Vol. 2009/2, *http://dx.doi.org/10.1787/fmt-v2009-art21-en*.

Blommestein, Hans J. (2006), *The growing importance of transparency in debt management and government securities markets*, 16th OECD Global Forum on Public Debt Management (Version: 30 November 2006), held on 6-7 December, 2006 in Amsterdam, The Netherlands.

Blommestein, Hans J. and Arzu Gok (2009), "OECD sovereign borrowing outlook 2009", *OECD Journal: Financial Market Trends*, Vol. 2009/1, *http://dx.doi.org/10.1787/fmt-v2009-art8-en*.

Blommestein, Hans J., O.S. Jensen and T. Olofsson (2010), "A Suggested New Approach to the Measurement and Reporting of Gross Short-Term Borrowing Operations by Governments", *OECD Journal: Financial Market Trends*, Vol. 2010/1, *http://dx.doi.org/10.1787/fmt-2010-5km7k9tnz6hd*.

Cebotary, A, (2008), "Contingent Liabilities: Issues and Practice", *IMF Working Paper* (WP/08/245), International Monetary Fund.

Cosio-Pascal, E. (2007), *Manual on Debt and Risk Indicators*, Inter-American Development Bank, Latin-American and Caribbean Debt Group, January, New York and Washington.

Eurostat, (2013), *Manual on Government Deficit and Debt – Implementation of ESA95*.

Fabozzi, Frank J. (2004), *The Handbook of European Fixed Income Securities*, John Wiley&Sons Inc., Hoboken, New Jersey.

International Monetary Fund, (2007), *Manual on Fiscal Transparency*.

OECD (2005), *Advances in Risk Management of Government Debt*, OECD Publishing, Paris, *http://dx.doi.org/10.1787/9789264104433-en*.

OECD (2002), "OECD Best Practices for Budget Transparency", *OECD Journal on Budgeting*, Vol. 1/3, *http://dx.doi.org/10.1787/budget-v1-art14-en*.

Phoa, W. (1998), *Advanced Fixed Income Analysis*, John Wiley&Sons Inc., New Hope, Pennsylvania.

Powell, Jerome H. (2015), "*Structure and Liquidity in Treasury Markets*", The Brookings Institution, 3 August 2015, Washington, DC, *www.federalreserve.gov/newsevents/speech/powell20150803a.htm*.

Standard & Poor's, (2008), *Sovereign Credit Ratings: A Primer*.

The Commonwealth Secretariat (2011), *Contingent Liabilities*, Meeting of Inter-Agency Task Force on Finance Statistics, London, United Kingdom, March.

World Bank, European Commission, IMF, OECD, UN, System of National Accounts 2008.

World Bank Institute (2013), *Disclosure of Project and Contract Information in Public-Private Partnerships*, International Bank for Reconstruction and Development.

World Bank Institute (2012), *Public-Private Partnerships Reference Guide*, Version 1.0, International Bank for Reconstruction and Development.

ANNEX 4.A1

Calculation of commonly used risk measures

Average Time to Maturity (ATM)

$$ATM = \frac{\sum_{t=1}^{n} t^{*}Pt}{\sum_{t=1}^{n} Pt}$$

where "Pt" is the principal amount of the maturing bond at time "t" and "n" is the number of the bond in portfolio.

Average Time to Re-Fixing (ATR)

$$ATR = \frac{\sum_{t=1}^{n} t * Pt}{\sum_{t=1}^{n} Pt}$$

where **Pt** is the principal amount whose interest rate is re-fixed at time **t** and **n** is the number of the bond in portfolio. **ATR** gives information about the exposure of the debt stock to changes in interest rates. The higher **ATR,** the lower this risk (for the issuer).

Macaulay Duration

For fixed coupon bonds the Macaulay Duration is calculated as follows:

$$Macaulay\,Duration = \frac{\sum_{t=1}^{k} t * PV(Ct)}{\sum_{t=1}^{k} PV(Ct)}$$

where **PV (Ct)** is the present value of the cash flow at time **t** (**Ct**). This measure takes into account both payments of interest and principal.

For zero-coupon securities, duration is equal to maturity. For variable (floating) rate bonds, duration is calculated as the time to the next interest rate fixing date.

Modified Duration

Modified Duration is calculated using the Macaulay Duration measure:

$$Modified\,Duration = Macaulay\,Duration * ((1 + i)^{-1})$$

where " **i** " is the yield to maturity of the bond.

Portfolio Duration

The duration of a portfolio can be calculated by calculating the weighted average of the duration of the bonds in the portfolio:

$$Portfolio\,Duration = D_1 * w_1 + D_2 * w_2 + \ldots + D_n * w_n$$

where $\mathbf{D_1, D_2, .. D_n}$ are the duration of the bonds in portfolio and $\mathbf{w_1, w_2, ..., w_n}$ are the weights of the bonds in the portfolio and **n** is the number of bonds in portfolio.

ORGANISATION FOR ECONOMIC CO-OPERATION AND DEVELOPMENT

The OECD is a unique forum where governments work together to address the economic, social and environmental challenges of globalisation. The OECD is also at the forefront of efforts to understand and to help governments respond to new developments and concerns, such as corporate governance, the information economy and the challenges of an ageing population. The Organisation provides a setting where governments can compare policy experiences, seek answers to common problems, identify good practice and work to co-ordinate domestic and international policies.

The OECD member countries are: Australia, Austria, Belgium, Canada, Chile, the Czech Republic, Denmark, Estonia, Finland, France, Germany, Greece, Hungary, Iceland, Ireland, Israel, Italy, Japan, Korea, Latvia, Luxembourg, Mexico, the Netherlands, New Zealand, Norway, Poland, Portugal, the Slovak Republic, Slovenia, Spain, Sweden, Switzerland, Turkey, the United Kingdom and the United States. The European Union takes part in the work of the OECD.

OECD Publishing disseminates widely the results of the Organisation's statistics gathering and research on economic, social and environmental issues, as well as the conventions, guidelines and standards agreed by its members.

OECD PUBLISHING, 2, rue André-Pascal, 75775 PARIS CEDEX 16
(20 2016 04 1 P) ISBN 978-92-64-25730-6 – 2016

www.ingramcontent.com/pod-product-compliance
Lightning Source LLC
LaVergne TN
LVHW081409110826
845149LV00010B/1685

* 9 7 8 9 2 6 4 2 5 7 3 0 6 *